# DATE DUE

| | | |
|---|---|---|
| DEC 03 2010 | | |
| MAY 09 2011 | | |
| AUG 23 2011 | | |
| OCT 21 2013 | | |
| APR 07 2017 | | |
| | | |
| DEC 11 2017 | | |
| | | |
| | | |
| | | |
| | | |
| | | |
| | | |
| | | |
| | | |
| | | |

# Personality Disorders

## Psychological Disorders

Psychological
Disorders

# Personality Disorders

Heather Barnett Veague, Ph.D.

Consulting Editor
**Christine Collins, Ph.D.**
Research Assistant
Professor of Psychology
Vanderbilt University

Foreword by
**Pat Levitt, Ph.D.**
Vanderbilt Kennedy
Center for Research
on Human Development

**CHELSEA HOUSE**
PUBLISHERS
An imprint of Infobase Publishing

**Personality Disorders**

Chelsea House
An imprint of Infobase Publishing
132 West 31st Street
New York NY 10001

ISBN-10: 0-7910-9002-7
ISBN-13: 978-0-7910-9002-2

**Library of Congress Cataloging-in-Publication Data**
Veague, Heather Barnett.
    Personality disorders / Heather Barnett Veague ; foreword by Pat Levitt.
        p. cm. — (Psychological disorders)
    Includes bibliographical references (p.    ) and index.
    ISBN 0-7910-9002-7 (hardcover)
    1.  Personality disorders. 2.  Psychotherapy.  I. Title. II. Series.
    RC555.P472 2007
    616.85'81—dc22                                        2006024072

Chelsea House books are available at special discounts when purchased in bulk quantities for businesses, associations, institutions, or sales promotions. Please call our Special Sales Department in New York at (212) 967-8800 or (800) 322-8755.

You can find Chelsea House on the World Wide Web at http://www.chelseahouse.com

Text and cover design by Keith Trego

Printed in the United States of America

Bang EJB 10 9 8 7 6 5 4 3 2

This book is printed on acid-free paper.

All links and Web addresses were checked and verified to be correct at the time of publication. Because of the dynamic nature of the Web, some addresses and links may have changed since publication and may no longer be valid.

# Table of Contents

## Foreword

**Pat Levitt, Ph.D.**
Vanderbilt Kennedy
Center for Research
on Human Development

**Think of the most complicated aspect of our universe, and then** multiply that by infinity! Even the most enthusiastic of mathematicians and physicists acknowledge that the brain is by far the most challenging entity to understand. By design, the human brain is made up of billions of cells called neurons, which use chemical neurotransmitters to communicate with each other through connections called synapses. Each brain cell has about 2,000 synapses. Connections between neurons are not formed in a random fashion, but rather, are organized into a type of architecture that is far more complex than any of today's supercomputers. And, not only is the brain's connective architecture more complex than any computer, its connections are capable of *changing* to improve the way a circuit functions. For example, the way we learn new information involves changes in circuits that actually improve performance. Yet some change can also result in a disruption of connections, like changes that occur in disorders such as drug addiction, depression, schizophrenia, and epilepsy, or even changes that can increase a person's risk of suicide.

Genes and the environment are powerful forces in building the brain during development and ensuring normal brain functioning, but they can also be the root causes of psychological and neurological disorders when things go awry. The way in which brain architecture is built before birth and in childhood will determine how well the brain functions when we are adults, and even how susceptible we are to such diseases as depression, anxiety, or attention disorders, which can severely disturb brain function. In a sense, then, understanding how the brain is built can lead us to a clearer picture of the ways in which our brain works, how we can improve its functioning, and what we can do to repair it when diseases strike.

Brain architecture reflects the highly specialized jobs that are performed by human beings, such as seeing, hearing, feeling, smelling, and moving. Different brain areas are specialized to control specific functions. Each specialized area must communicate well with other areas for the brain to accomplish even more complex tasks, like controlling body physiology—our patterns of sleep, for example, or even our eating habits, both of which can become disrupted if brain development or function is disturbed in some way. The brain controls our feelings, fears, and emotions; our ability to learn and store new information; and how well we recall old information. The brain does all this, and more, by building, during development, the circuits that control these functions, much like a hard-wired computer. Even small abnormalities that occur during early brain development through gene mutations, viral infection, or fetal exposure to alcohol can increase the risk of developing a wide range of psychological disorders later in life.

Those who study the relationship between brain architecture and function, and the diseases that affect this bond, are neuroscientists. Those who study and treat the disorders that are caused by changes in brain architecture and chemistry are psychiatrists and psychologists. Over the last 50 years, we have learned quite a lot about how brain architecture and chemistry work and how genetics contribute to brain structure and function. Genes are very important in controlling the initial phases of building the brain. In fact, almost every gene in the human genome is needed to build the brain. This process of brain development actually starts prior to birth, with almost all the neurons we will ever have in our brain produced by mid-gestation. The assembly of the architecture, in the form of intricate circuits, begins by this time, and by birth, we have the basic organization laid out. But the work is not yet complete, because billions of connections form over a remarkably long period of time, extending through puberty. The brain of a child is being built and modified on a daily basis, even during sleep.

While there are thousands of chemical building blocks, such as proteins, lipids, and carbohydrates, that are used, much like bricks and mortar, to put the architecture together, the highly detailed connectivity that emerges during childhood depends greatly upon experiences and our environment. In building a house, we use specific blueprints to assemble the basic structures, like a foundation, walls, floors, and ceilings. The brain is assembled similarly. Plumbing and electricity, like the basic circuitry of the brain, are put in place early in the building process. But for all of this early work, there is another very important phase of development, which is termed experience-dependent development. During the first three years of life, our brains actually form far more connections than we will ever need, almost 40% more! Why would this occur? Well, in fact, the early circuits form in this way so that we can use experience to mold our brain architecture to best suit the functions that we are likely to need for the rest of our lives.

Experience is not just important for the circuits that control our senses. A young child who experiences toxic stress, like physical abuse, will have his or her brain architecture changed in regions that will result in poorer control of emotions and feelings as an adult. Experience is powerful. When we repeatedly practice on the piano or shoot a basketball hundreds of times daily, we are using experience to model our brain connections to function at their finest. Some will achieve better results than others, perhaps because the initial phases of circuit-building provided a better base, just like the architecture of houses may differ in terms of their functionality. We are working to understand the brain structure and function that result from the powerful combination of genes building the initial architecture and a child's experience adding the all-important detailed touches. We also know that, like an old home, the architecture can break down. The aging process can be particularly hard on the ability of brain circuits to function at their best because positive change comes less readily as we get older. Synapses may be lost and brain chemistry can change over time. The difficulties in understanding how architecture gets built are paralleled by the complexities of what happens to that architecture as we grow older. Dementia associated with brain deterioration as a complication of Alzheimer's disease, or memory loss associated with aging or alcoholism are active avenues of research in the neuroscience community.

There is truth, both for development and in aging, in the old adage "use it or lose it." Neuroscientists are pursuing the idea that brain architecture and chemistry can be modified well beyond childhood. If we understand the mechanisms that make it easy for a young, healthy brain to learn or repair itself following an accident, perhaps we can use those same tools to optimize the functioning of aging brains. We already know many ways in which we can improve the functioning of the aging or injured brain. For example, for an individual who has suffered a stroke that has caused structural damage to brain architecture, physical exercise can be quite powerful in helping to reorganize circuits so that they function better, even in an elderly individual. And you know that when you exercise and sleep regularly, you just feel better. Your brain chemistry and architecture are functioning at their best. Another example of ways we can improve nervous system function are the drugs that are used to treat mental illnesses. These drugs are designed to change brain chemistry so that the neurotransmitters used for communication between brain cells can function more normally. These same types of drugs, however, when taken in excess or abused, can actually damage brain chemistry and change brain architecture so that it functions more poorly.

As you read the series Psychological Disorders, the images of altered brain organization and chemistry will come to mind in thinking about complex diseases such as schizophrenia or drug addiction. There is nothing more fascinating and important to understand for the well-being of humans. But also keep in mind that as neuroscientists, we are on a mission to comprehend human nature, the way we perceive the world, how we recognize color, why we smile when thinking about the Thanksgiving turkey, the emotion of experiencing our first kiss, or how we can remember the winner of the 1953 World Series. If you are interested in people, and the world in which we live, you are a neuroscientist, too.

Pat Levitt, Ph.D.
Director, Vanderbilt Kennedy Center
for Research on Human Development
Vanderbilt University
Nashville, Tennessee

# An Overview

**The way a person thinks, feels, and behaves makes up his or her** personality. We all have personality traits. You might be easygoing or happy-go-lucky. Alternatively you might be shy or quiet. In any case, you have personality traits that help you decide how to respond to different situations. Some people have personality traits that cause them to respond to situations in ways that cause them problems. They might act afraid of all new situations or act without thinking of the consequences of their behavior. When someone's personality causes them problems at work and at home we say that they have a **personality disorder.**

If you were asked to describe your classmates, you might think of how they interact with you or with others: "Kevin is easy to get along with;" "Caitlyn likes to help people;" "Michael is often jealous of other people;" "Katie is very sensitive and cries easily." Usually, the way someone behaves differs from one situation to another. For example, Caitlyn might really enjoy helping others at school but not enjoy helping her younger brother with his homework. However, the behavior of people with personality disorders tends to be rigid. That is, the way they think, feel, and behave remains the same from one situation to another.

Currently, one of the most popular theories describing the structure of personality is the **Five-Factor Theory.**[1] The Five-Factor Theory comes from research into the personality traits of

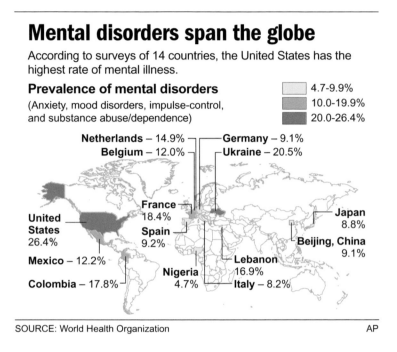

## Mental disorders span the globe

According to surveys of 14 countries, the United States has the highest rate of mental illness.

**Prevalence of mental disorders**

(Anxiety, mood disorders, impulse-control, and substance abuse/dependence)

- 4.7-9.9%
- 10.0-19.9%
- 20.0-26.4%

Netherlands – 14.9%
Belgium – 12.0%
Germany – 9.1%
Ukraine – 20.5%
France 18.4%
United States 26.4%
Spain 9.2%
Japan 8.8%
Beijing, China 9.1%
Mexico – 12.2%
Lebanon 16.9%
Nigeria 4.7%
Italy – 8.2%
Colombia – 17.8%

SOURCE: World Health Organization                                    AP

**Figure 1.1** © *AP Images*

people all over the world. People are rated on five factors (or dimensions): extroversion, agreeableness, conscientiousness, emotional stability, and openness to experience. Remember that these factors are dimensions, meaning that everyone exhibits each factor to a greater or lesser degree or amount. Indeed, people vary continuously on these factors and most people fall somewhere in the middle, between the extremes. Within the Five-Factor model, people are rated on each dimension as high, low, or somewhere in the middle. It appears that the factors are stable over a long period of time, beginning in early adulthood. This means that if you are a very easygoing child, you will most likely be a very easygoing adult. These factors also appear to be **heritable**, or passed down between generations. Finally, the factors are considered universal, having been investigated in non-English-speaking cultures. This means that people in Asia and Africa have the same personality traits as do people in the United States and Canada.

## Five-Factor Model of Personality

One of the most popular approaches among psychologists for studying personality traits is the "Five-Factor Model" of personality. According to the "Five-Factor Model," personality is made up of a combination of five factors, or traits:

- Neuroticism: Neuroticism is the tendency to feel bad. Someone who scores highly on neuroticism may frequently feel anxious or sad.

- Extroversion: "Extroversion" could also be called "outgoingness." Someone who scores high on extroversion enjoys being with other people and usually feels happy.

- Openness to experience: Openness to experience includes being curious about the world and open to new ideas.

- Agreeableness: Agreeableness is measured by how likely you are to feel compassion for someone. Someone who scores highly on agreeableness is generally concerned about other people.

- Conscientiousness: Conscientiousness is defined as being organized, focused, and goal-oriented.

*Source*: Adapted from Costa, P. T., Jr., and R. R. McCrae. "Personality Disorders and the Five-Factor Model of Personality." *Journal of Personality Disorders* 4 (1990): 362–371.

## DIMENSIONS VERSUS CATEGORIES

Psychological researchers have various theories about the ways in which characteristics of personality disorders differ from what we would consider "normal" personality traits. Some researchers believe that symptoms of personality disorders could be considered normal responses to a given situation, except for one crucial difference: the intensity of the response. For example, at times, we all have felt suspicious of others, extremely self-confident, stubborn, or moody. For most of us, these experiences come and go without causing significant problems in our daily lives. But someone with a personality disorder may experience these normal feelings with much greater intensity than normal. Researchers and clinicians will explain this by saying that there is a **quantitative** rather than **qualitative** difference in their experience.

A **dimensional model** of personality assumes that everyone displays the same personality traits, but some people experience them to a greater intensity than others. For example, all of us have felt shy at some time. Someone who is extremely shy, so much that shyness significantly interferes with life, might be diagnosed with **avoidant personality disorder**. Alternatively, someone who never displays shyness and is only comfortable when they are the center of attention might be diagnosed with **histrionic personality disorder**. A dimensional model of personality disorders suggests that people with personality disorders differ in the *degree* of the emotional or behavioral experience, rather than in the *kind* of emotional experience.

Other researchers argue that people with personality disorders exhibit thoughts and behaviors that are qualitatively different from normal thoughts and behaviors. These researchers take a **categorical approach** to personality disorders. As human beings, we learn to separate the people or objects in our world into categories at a very young age. A simple example of a category we use daily is gender. We view a person as falling into only one category of gender: either a man *or* a woman, a boy *or* a girl. Another category we use is height. Usually, we describe someone as tall or short.

Although most researchers and clinicians agree that personality disorders are disorders of intensity (the dimensional model), diagnosing a disorder means putting someone into a category. If someone reports or demonstrates several symptoms of a disorder, he or she generally receives that diagnosis. For example, in order to receive a diagnosis of **borderline personality disorder**, a patient must exhibit five out of nine symptoms. Someone who has five of those symptoms receives the same diagnosis as someone who has nine of the symptoms (though at a lesser degree). However, someone who reports only four symptoms would not receive the diagnosis. This presents a dilemma to both clinicians and researchers. Imagine the following situation: You are a psychologist evaluating three clients. Your first client reports that she experiences four symptoms of borderline personality disorder. The second client reports experiencing five symptoms of borderline personality disorder. The third client reports experiencing nine symptoms of borderline personality disorder. The first and second clients might seem very similar in that they report nearly the same types and degree of difficulty in their social and emotional lives. However, the first client does not report enough symptoms (five) to qualify for the diagnosis. Alternatively, the second and third clients receive the same diagnosis, even if the third client seems to have a lot more problems than the second.

Another problem in diagnosis is **heterogeneity** (difference of kind) within a category. Consider borderline personality disorder. A person must experience at least five out of nine symptoms or signs to receive the diagnosis. This means that any two people who receive the diagnosis of borderline personality disorder

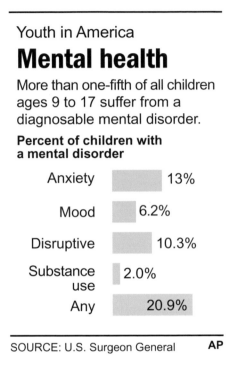

Youth in America

# Mental health

More than one-fifth of all children
ages 9 to 17 suffer from a
diagnosable mental disorder.

**Percent of children with
a mental disorder**

Anxiety        13%

Mood        6.2%

Disruptive        10.3%

Substance        2.0%
use

Any        20.9%

SOURCE: U.S. Surgeon General        **AP**

**Figure 1.2** © *AP Images*

might share only one symptom. Thus, two people might exhibit very different symptoms yet still fall under the same diagnosis. When there are a lot of differences between people within a
category, that category is considered heterogeneous.

### HOW DO YOU DECIDE IF SOMEONE HAS A PERSONALITY DISORDER?

**Personality disorders** are made up of ways of viewing and thinking about oneself and others that do not change much from one
day to the next. Additionally, these perceptions, thoughts, and
behaviors are upsetting to the individual who experiences them,

or they cause problems in the individual's personal relationships. If a person's characteristic ways of interacting with others cause significant problems in her life, and if she is unable to change these behaviors, we might say that this person has a personality disorder.

Personality disorders are different from other types of mental disorders you may have studied, such as depression or schizophrenia. Personality disorders tend to be chronic and long-lasting. One way to think of a personality disorder is to liken it to a disease like diabetes. Someone with diabetes always has diabetes and takes medicine everyday to help him control his symptoms. A different, more temporary kind of sickness is a cold. When you get a cold, you might have symptoms like a runny nose and cough for a few days or even a few weeks. Likewise, someone with major depression might have depressive symptoms for a few weeks but will eventually feel better. A person with depression might suffer a major depressive episode that lasts a few weeks or months, while an individual with a personality disorder must deal with their problems for years. In fact, one requirement for diagnosis of a personality disorder is that the characteristic behavior patterns of a patient with a personality disorder must be able to be traced back to adolescence or early adulthood. For example, an adult man with a personality disorder may experience feelings of shyness, inadequacy, and acute sensitivity to negative feedback in nearly all situations. He might remember feeling very uncomfortable in school and afraid of being criticized by his teachers or classmates. To avoid these negative feelings, perhaps he pretended to be sick and stayed home from school. Now, as a young adult, he might say that he feels as insecure at a small party with friends as he does in a large meeting at his job. Because of his feelings of inadequacy, he may avoid situations in which he is required to interact with others, and might prefer a job where he works alone and has limited social interactions.

One of the criteria for diagnosing a personality disorder is that the pattern of behavior leads to "clinically significant impairment in functioning." This means that the pattern of behavior causes serious problems in one's life. In the case of the man with avoidant personality disorder described above, it is

## DSM-IV-TR's Five Criteria

Researchers and clinicians use a definition of personality disorders that is found in the American Psychiatric Association's *Diagnostic and Statistical Manual of Mental Disorders* (DSM-IV-TR). According to the DSM, the essential feature of a personality disorder is a long-lasting pattern of thought and behavior that is different from most other people in the same culture. Someone is diagnosed with a personality disorder if he meets the following criteria:

1. Personality problems are present in at least two of the following areas: thoughts, emotions, personal relationships, or behaviors.

2. The patient has experienced personality problems in most parts of his life, including at work, at school, and at home.

3. The problems caused by the personality disorder are upsetting to the patient or frequently cause problems in his relations with other people.

4. The patient's personality problems typically begin in the teenage years and continue throughout adulthood.

5. The personality disturbance is not due to drugs or alcohol, nor is it due to the presence of another illness.

clear that his work and social life are affected by his disorder. First, he is limited in what kind of job he can take. Second, he finds it very difficult to make friends. Many young men feel nervous asking someone out on a date, but for a man with avoidant personality disorder, it is nearly impossible. Individuals with avoidant personality disorder *want* to have relationships with other people but are paralyzed by their shyness and fear of interacting with others. Their shyness often causes them to feel isolated and lonely, which may be considered "significant distress."

Sometimes, personality disorders do not cause the affected person distress. Occasionally, someone with a personality disorder lacks **insight** into his or her illness. This means that the person cannot understand that his or her thoughts and behaviors are harmful or maladaptive. The diagnostic criteria allow a clinician to diagnose a personality disorder if the clinician can determine that other people feel distress as a result of the affected individual's behavior. This is particularly true for people diagnosed with **antisocial personality disorder**, a condition in which individuals show a "blatant disregard for the rights of others yet exhibit no remorse." In this situation, a clinician must determine whether the behaviors are disruptive enough to cause significant problems for other people.

## AXIS I VERSUS AXIS II

The American Psychiatric Association (APA) uses the axis system to distinguish between acute, or cyclical, disorders like depression or schizophrenia, and chronic personality disorders. In psychiatric terms, the axes refer to categories into which all mental disorders fall. Most psychological disorders, including mood disorders, schizophrenia, eating disorders, and anxiety disorders, fall within the Axis I classification of disorders. These disorders are categorized together in Axis I because they share certain qualities, namely a tendency to be cyclical (come and go). Because personality disorders are considered qualitatively different from these other types of mental illness—namely, they are stable rather than cyclical—personality disorders are placed on a different axis, Axis II. When someone seeks help from a clinician, her symptoms are considered in order to determine whether she has a current acute disorder (Axis I) or a more chronic personality disorder (Axis II). These axes are not mutually exclusive. That is, just because a person has a disorder on one axis does not mean she cannot meet the criteria for a disorder on another axis. In fact, it is not uncommon for a person to meet the criteria for a disorder on each axis. For example, someone with a personality disorder might also have a diagnosis of depression. In addition, one might meet criteria for more than one disorder on either axis. In such cases, the work of a clinician becomes particularly challenging.

## CATEGORIES OF PERSONALITY DISORDERS

Personality disorders are grouped into three **clusters** (**A**, **B**, and **C**) based upon similarities among them. It is not unusual for a person to receive a diagnosis of more than one personality disorder because of the frequency of shared symptoms.

### Cluster A: The Odd Cluster

People with Cluster A disorders may be described as withdrawn, distant, cold, or suspicious. These disorders include **paranoid**, **schizoid**, and **schizotypal personality disorders**. As a kind of informal, "shorthand" way of remembering what Cluster A personality disorders are like, we can call them the "weird" cluster.

### Cluster B: The Impulsive Cluster

People with Cluster B disorders may be described as dramatic, emotional, and attention-seeking. They may seem to be "moody" or "difficult." These individuals often report that they have difficulty getting along with others. These disorders include **antisocial, borderline, histrionic,** and **narcissistic personality disorders.** To make Cluster B personality disorders easy to remember, we can call these disorders the "wild" cluster.

### Cluster C: The Anxious Cluster
People with Cluster C disorders may be described as tense, anxious, or uptight. These disorders include **avoidant, dependent,** and **obsessive-compulsive personality disorders.** We can call Cluster C disorders the "worried" cluster.

These disorders will be described in detail in later chapters. For now, the "3 Ws" may be a helpful way of remembering which disorder falls into which cluster: "the weird" (A), "the wild" (B), and "the worried" (C). People who demonstrate Cluster A disorders may seem strange, weird, odd, or eccentric, demonstrating unusual behavior that ranges from suspiciousness to social isolation. In Cluster B, we find individuals who tend to be dramatic, emotional, and erratic, often demonstrating "wild" behavior. Cluster C people are anxious, often "worried" about everything, from relationships and financial security to the tidiness and organization of their home.

Two additional personality disorders are currently being considered by the American Psychiatric Association to be included in the DSM: **depressive** and **passive aggressive personality disorders.** Later in the text, we will discuss what is known and what still needs to be known about depressive and passive aggressive personality disorders.

Personality disorders are fairly rare. These disorders are found in only 0.5 percent to 2.5 percent of the general population of the United States, meaning that out of 100 people, fewer than three will exhibit enough symptoms to be diagnosed with

**Table 1.1** Summary of Personality Disorders

| PERSONALITY DISORDER | SYMPTOMS OR SIGNS | PREVALENCE IN THE UNITED STATES | GENDER |
|---|---|---|---|
| **Cluster A** | | | |
| Paranoid | Suspiciousness of others | 0.5–2.5% | males>females |
| Schizoid | Inability to form and lack of interest in social relationships | <1% | males>females |
| Schizotypal | Strange thought patterns, magical thinking, odd perceptions | 3% | males>females |
| **Cluster B** | | | |
| Histrionic | Tendency to be overly emotional and dramatic | 2–3% | males=females |
| Narcissistic | Overly self-involved, views self as special and deserves special attention | <1% | males>females |
| Antisocial | Deceitful, manipulates people, history of conduct problems in childhood | 1% females 3% males | males>females |
| Borderline | Moody, fears abandonment, feels empty, self-mutilates, or attempts suicide | 2% | males<females |
| **Cluster C** | | | |
| Avoidant | Very sensitive to interpersonal rejection | 0.5–1% | males=females |
| Dependent | Has difficulty being alone, doesn't like to end relationships, will do unpleasant things in order to keep people around, such as volunteer to do all house cleaning | 2% | males=females |
| Obsessive | Excessive concern with details, orderliness, and rules; difficulty relaxing and having fun | 1% | males>females |

a personality disorder. It is tempting to diagnose oneself or others when you learn about a mental disorder. There are two things you need to remember: (1) Diagnosis is a complicated discipline, requiring careful training and practice. Even experienced clinicians and researchers often disagree about an individual's diagnosis. (2) Personality disorders are diagnosed in adults, not in children or teenagers. Adolescence can be a confusing and complicated time biologically and socially, during which some young people experience unusually intense thoughts, emotions, or behaviors. For these reasons, you should try not to identify these categories in yourself or other people. However, if you do recognize harmful behaviors that you or someone you know has exhibited, it is important to speak with a parent, teacher, or counselor.

# 2

# The "Odd" Cluster

**I've always felt closer to animals than to people. Birds just seem** to understand me. My favorite time of year is the spring, when the robins return for the summer. I have a favorite robin who comes back every year. I know he comes just for me. That's why I can't ever leave New York. I can't talk about my feelings for animals because people think I'm strange. I want to have friends, but most people don't have my special gifts. They either can't understand me or are jealous, I'm not sure which. I get pretty sad sometimes, and feel lonely, but I know that I'm lucky. I've been chosen. I have a gift.

—Donald, a 32-year-old man diagnosed
with schizotypal personality disorder

This chapter will discuss the features of three personality disorders that are included in Cluster A, the "odd" cluster that includes paranoid, schizoid, and schizotypal personality disorders. People with Cluster A disorders exhibit behaviors that alienate them from others. They experience thoughts about other people that make it difficult for them to be in relationships, and they tend to view the world as threatening or dangerous. Some research suggests that there is overlap between schizophrenia and schizotypal personality disorder in particular. However, you should recall that personality disorders are different from Axis I disorders like schizophrenia in that personality disorders are chronic while schizophrenia appears to be cyclical. That is, symptoms of schizophrenia may come and go, whereas symptoms of "odd" cluster personality disorders are usually long-lasting. The Cluster A personality disorders that will be discussed in this chapter are paranoid personality disorder, schizoid personality disorder, and schizotypal personality disorder.

## PARANOID PERSONALITY DISORDER

The essential feature of **paranoid personality disorder** (PPD) is a pattern of pervasive distrust and suspiciousness of others. People with PPD often believe that others are behaving in a way that is dishonest or that others are out to get them. PPD sufferers believe that other people intend to hurt or take advantage of them, even if there is no evidence that this is true. They cannot trust others and often believe that others are plotting against them, or might attack them at any time. They constantly question the motives of their colleagues, family, and friends, and doubt their loyalty and trustworthiness. Confiding in others is difficult because they worry that any personal information they share will be used against them. Individuals with PPD often interpret everyday conversations or comments as having negative or malicious intent. They may view neutral comments as hostile or threatening. Sometimes, people with PPD hold grudges. They have trouble "forgiving and forgetting." It can be especially difficult for someone who is married to an individual with PPD because the PPD sufferer may question the loyalty of his or her spouse. The PPD patient may constantly suspect that his or her partner is cheating, even if there is no evidence to support that suspicion.

As you might imagine, individuals with paranoid personality disorder have significant problems in their social relationships. Their suspiciousness may cause them to be argumentative and/or hostile. Sometimes, people with PPD act very distant and cold. They avoid other people because they are constantly questioning people's motives. In so doing, these individuals might start a cycle of hostility that confirms their negative expectations of others. That is, because these people often respond to others with anger, others might also react with hostility, thus confirming the original expectation that others are "out to get them."

**CASE STUDY: PARANOID PERSONALITY DISORDER**

Steven is a 30-year-old mailroom clerk in a large law firm in Los Angeles. He is ambivalent about his job. He enjoys the time he spends sorting mail but dislikes the time he must spend chatting with the attorneys and secretaries on the upper floors. He believes that the secretaries are laughing at him when he drops off the mail. There is one secretary in particular whom Steven dislikes. Every day when he drops off the mail, she is on the phone. Steven thinks that she is talking to the president of the law firm about him, trying to get him fired.

Steven has always had problems trusting others. In elementary school, he had very few friends. He believed that the teachers and most of the other children didn't like him and were making fun of him when he wasn't there. Because of his discomfort, he was often absent from school. When he stayed home from school, he worried that the teacher and students were talking about him, planning to embarrass him when he came back. His parents were divorced, but Steven spent equal time with both parents. He felt close to his mother, but believed that his father left their home because he was disappointed in Steven. Whenever he was at his dad's house, he spent most of his time in his room reading or writing science-fiction stories.

As an adult, Steven is a "loner." He rarely dates, because he thinks women are just using him. When he does go out with women, he often wonders whether they really like him or if they just like the fact that he takes them to the movies or dinner. He has one friend, John, a young man who is part of a group of people who believe that the government is corrupt and so they are preparing for a civil war. Steven and John enjoy studying antique firearms and participating in Civil War reenactments that they believe are preparing them for the battles of the future.

It is difficult for a clinician to get to know Steven. Steven claims to "read between the lines" of the interview questions and thinks that the clinician wants to have him hospitalized

**Figure 2.1** People suffering from paranoid personality disorder often avoid contact with others, preferring to remain "loners." © *John Henley/CORBIS*

against his will. Steven offers very little information and is on guard throughout the interview.

People with paranoid personality disorder need to be self-sufficient and independent because of their problems interacting with others. These people tend to be very controlling of their environment and may be seen as rigid or critical of others. Usually, someone with PPD will choose a job where he may work alone, like Steven who works in a mailroom. These people are often litigious—that is, they take other people to court because they blame others for their problems. They might view the world in stereotypes, assigning motives to groups of people based on physical, ethnic, or political associations. Finally, people with PPD are often most comfortable with others who share their suspicious view of the world. For example, Steven is comfortable with his friend John because John also believes that people are not to be trusted. Thus, many people with PPD are fanatics or join cults that keep them apart from the rest of society.

It is often difficult to determine whether someone has PPD because his paranoid beliefs may sound real. People with paranoid personality disorder typically exhibit overvalued ideas. That is, their ideas may or may not be true and are not delusions. Delusions are often complicated and bizarre (for example, being abducted by aliens and taken aboard a spaceship), but overvalued ideas are not obviously false but continue to be held in spite of evidence that they are incorrect (for example, having a cheating spouse). People with PPD might occasionally experience brief psychotic episodes. This means that they may lose touch with reality, as individuals with schizophrenia do, but it only occurs for a few minutes or hours. These episodes may occur when the person is under particular stress, such as having to work with a lot of people. Additionally, people with PPD often experience major depressive disorder, agoraphobia, obsessive-compulsive disorder, or alcohol/drug abuse.

In childhood, problems associated with paranoid personality disorder might appear as underachievement, isolation, or being very sensitive to criticism. As with Steven, who believed that his teacher and classmates were laughing at him behind his back, many adults with PPD recall that even when they were children they suspected that others were out to get them. Males are much more likely than females to be diagnosed with paranoid personality disorder. As with most personality disorders, PPD is rare and affects between 0.5 and 2.5 percent of the population of the United States. It is more common in psychiatric hospitals, where between 10 and 30 percent of psychiatric patients have PPD.

## SCHIZOID PERSONALITY DISORDER

Individuals with schizoid personality disorder (SPD) are detached from other people and prefer to be alone. As a result, someone with SPD will usually choose solitary activities. He or she may prefer playing solitary computer games or working on math problems to playing sports or games or being with others. Although you might enjoy going to the beach and putting your feet in the ocean or eating an ice cream cone, someone with schizoid personality disorder tends to get very little pleasure from sensory experiences like these. They exhibit a restricted range of affect, meaning that they usually don't display emotions. Finally, a hallmark of schizoid personality disorder is the complete lack of any close friends or confidants. Other than a first-degree relative, such as a parent or sibling, these people rarely maintain any close relationships.

### CASE STUDY: SCHIZOID PERSONALITY DISORDER

Randy is a 40-year-old computer programmer. He works for a small Internet company, and chooses to work at night, when he is one of only two people in the office. He rarely leaves his cubicle. He eats alone at his desk, and never speaks to the other person in the office.

Randy is very good at his job. He is detail-oriented, responsible, and enjoys the challenge of computer programming. His boss, Mr. Simms, would like to promote Randy because of Randy's skill and hard work, but he hesitates to do so because of Randy's personality. To others, Randy seems very stiff and cold. He doesn't make good eye contact and never laughs at people's jokes. Mr. Simms's hesitation to promote him makes little difference to Randy. If he were offered the promotion, he probably wouldn't take it. Randy does not want to supervise others. He doesn't want to have to talk to people any more than necessary. Besides, his current salary is sufficient to support him in his quiet, solitary life.

Randy has always preferred to be alone. As a child, he was the only son with two younger sisters. Although his sisters were popular and were involved in several activities in school, Randy was always considered a "computer nerd." He spent all his time at home, building his own computer and working on math problems. He did have one friend in high school, James, who was interested in computers, too, and liked to play role-playing games. After high school, James and Randy went their separate ways and Randy never found another friend.

Randy has never dated and is not interested in getting married. Women have approached him, but he is so uncomfortable around them that he usually just mumbles an excuse and leaves. He recognizes that he is different from other people. Randy sees that others have relationships and seem happy and comfortable in groups. Sometimes, he thinks he should see a therapist about his isolation, but making such a visit would require too much effort. After all, he would have to call to make an appointment, then actually talk to another person for an hour. That seems much too daunting! For now, he'll continue to work, alone, with his computer.

---

You might think that Randy or other individuals with SPD sound extremely shy. However, schizoid personality disorder may be distinguished from shyness by the patient's lack of interest in the opinions of others. People with SPD do not care what others think of them. In general, they are unskilled in social situations. Their social awkwardness may cause them to appear superficial or self-absorbed. In reality, these individuals are probably not good at noticing other people's social, interpersonal, or emotional cues. Because they exhibit a restricted emotional range, they may appear "bland," and they rarely smile or nod. Anger is a real problem for individuals with SPD. Even when provoked, these individuals rarely express anger or rage. Their lives may appear unfocused, as though they don't have a goal or a plan. They usually have no friends, don't date, and rarely marry. Although they have problems working with others, people with schizoid personality disorder can excel in solitary jobs. For instance, Randy does very well in his night job as a computer programmer because he has almost no interactions with other people.

As with paranoid personality disorder, individuals with schizoid personality disorder might experience very brief psychotic episodes in response to stress. Unlike paranoid personality disorder, however, individuals with SPD typically do not believe that other people intend to harm them. Whereas individuals with paranoid personality disorder rarely interact with others because they don't trust other people, individuals with SPD rarely interact with others because they are indifferent to interpersonal relationships.

**Figure 2.2** Children can experience symptoms of schizoid personality disorder and many other personality disorders. © *Lightscapes Photography, Inc./CORBIS*

Aspects of schizoid personality disorder may be observed in children, although children cannot be diagnosed with a personality disorder. Children who might develop this disorder as adults are often "loners," do not have many friends, may not do well in school, and may be teased by other children. There is little information available about how many people in the United States suffer from schizoid personality disorder. This might be because affected individuals are not usually bothered by their symptoms enough to seek clinical help. What we do know is that the disorder appears to be more common in males than females. Overall, SPD appears to affect less than 1 percent of the population of the United States.

**SCHIZOTYPAL PERSONALITY DISORDER**
Like people with schizoid and paranoid personality disorders, individuals with **schizotypal personality disorder** (sometimes

called *borderline schizophrenia* or *latent schizophrenia*) also experience social and interpersonal problems. In addition to their social and interpersonal impairment, however, people with schizotypal personality disorder experience cognitive distortions, have peculiar ways of thinking about the world, and exhibit eccentric behavior.

## CASE STUDY: SCHIZOTYPAL PERSONALITY DISORDER

Michael always felt like he was halfway between this world and the next. Even as a child he felt different. When he played outside, he believed that the squirrels would stop what they were doing and stare at him. He took this to mean that he could communicate with small animals, and that "Mother Nature" was sending him signals. He told his mother about his beliefs, and she told him that his Aunt Barbara had similar abilities. She called it a "gift." Over time, he felt more and more isolated from his peers. Michael found it very difficult to communicate with other children his age. Sometimes he wished that he didn't have this "gift." He just wanted to be a normal kid.

As an adult, Michael was frequently depressed. He lived at home with his mother and worked part-time in a video store. He was very interested in old Westerns and watched them over and over again while he was at work. The heroes in the old movies fascinated him. They were quietly brave and everyone feared them. He wished he could be like one of the characters in his movies—then people would respect him and want to spend time with him. Michael wanted to go out on dates and have a girlfriend, but he seemed to have trouble connecting with women. When he would go out with someone, he was often distracted by his date's hand gestures. He wondered if she was trying to send him a message by the way she used her hands. Michael didn't have many friends, even though he was interested in other people. Ideally, he wanted to meet more people who shared his "gift," since they might be better able to understand him.

When Michael was 28 years old, he decided to see a therapist for his depression. The therapist found his speech vague and difficult to follow. Michael was not psychotic, but his thinking was slightly disorganized. He was guarded, but it was difficult to determine whether he was shy or suspicious. Ultimately, Michael told his therapist that he feels that he has a "special mission" in life but he isn't sure what it is. He is very unhappy and wants to understand why he is so different from other people.

---

The cognitive distortions that Michael and other individuals with schizotypal personality disorder typically experience are frequently extreme manifestations of superstitious behaviors. An example of this is an idea of reference, or a belief that everyday events have special significance for them personally. An example of an **idea of reference** is the belief that by stepping on a crack in the sidewalk, you will cause some sort of harm to someone. As children, many of us heard the phrase "step on a crack, break your mother's back," but few of us take it literally. People with STPD often believe that they possess special powers, just as Michael believes he can communicate with animals. Other people with STPD may be very superstitious or preoccupied with paranormal activity (ghosts or spirits, for example). They might believe that they are clairvoyant, meaning they can see the future. Sometimes these individuals believe that they have magical control over others. An example of this would be thinking that your friend is going to call you, and then he or she calls you 15 minutes later. People with STPD might dismiss the explanation that this is merely a coincidence, instead believing that their thoughts summoned the phone call. Finally, individuals with STPD might experience **perceptual alterations**. For example, they might sense that another person is in the room or they might hear someone whispering their name.

People with schizotypal personality disorder are often suspicious of others. They are unskilled socially, and often fail to pick up on others' social cues. Because they are socially awkward, they might be viewed as inappropriate or stiff. They often exhibit odd mannerisms and avoid making eye contact with others. Individuals with STPD often use **idiosyncratic** language to describe everyday things. They might choose words that are extremely abstract, like describing what they do as an "endeavor." Alternatively, they might choose words that are extremely concrete, such as saying that two people who are married are "webbed." Their peculiar behavior and lack of social skills make others uncomfortable around them and, in turn, they are generally awkward around others. Unlike individuals with paranoid or schizoid personality disorder, individuals with STPD might say that their lack of interpersonal relationships bothers them. That is, they want to feel connected to others but have a difficult time making social connections. Although Michael would like to have a girlfriend, he has difficulty feeling comfortable around women. In social situations, STPD patients tend to feel extremely anxious. Unlike most people who become more comfortable in a social situation as time passes, individuals with STPD are likely to enter a social situation anxious and remain anxious throughout the event. For example, they might choose to attend a dinner party, but they will feel more uncomfortable and increasingly suspicious of others as the night goes on.

Individuals with schizotypal personality disorder often experience episodes of major depression or anxiety. In fact, it is often the depression or anxiety that leads these people to seek treatment, rather than the symptoms of STPD. Because these individuals are likely to seek treatment, researchers are able to estimate the prevalence of this disorder with more certainty than paranoid or schizoid personality disorders. It appears that STPD appears in about 3 percent of the population of the United States, and it is more common in males than in females.

## What Is a "Schizotype"?

Some research has revealed a genetic and biological association between schizophrenia and schizotypal personality disorder. Indeed, schizophrenia and schizotypal personality disorder often appear together in families. This means that individuals with schizophrenia are likely to have relatives with schizotypal personality disorder, and vice versa: Individuals with schizotypal personality disorder are likely to have relatives with schizophrenia. Research suggests that there is a series of genes that contain information about an inherited trait, and this series of genes (known as a genotype) may influence the development of schizophrenia or schizotypal personality disorder. Some researchers consider schizotypal personality disorder to be one possible outcome of the schizophrenia genotype. This means that given the same genotype, some people might develop schizophrenia, some may develop schizotypal personality disorder, and some may develop no symptoms at all. Environmental influences—such as the mother's being ill while she is pregnant with the child, or family stress during childhood—are thought to uniquely affect individuals with the schizophrenia genotype and increase the likelihood of schizophrenia symptoms.

Childhood signs of schizotypal personality disorder are a lot like the early signs of the other Cluster A disorders. These children might appear to be "loners," having few social relationships, experiencing intense social anxiety, and being hypersensitive to criticism. Furthermore, these children might exhibit odd fantasies and use peculiar language, qualities that might lead their peers to tease them.

Historically, researchers called people who had the schizophrenia genotype, "schizotypes." A schizotype was someone who had schizophrenia in his family, regardless of whether or not he showed schizophrenia symptoms himself. In the 1990s, research by Mark Lenzenweger at the State University of New York at Binghamton suggested that schizotypal personality disorder actually has more in common with schizophrenia than it does with personality disorders.[2] In fact, several studies have found that individuals with schizotypal personality disorder have the same cognitive difficulties (problems in thinking) that individuals with schizophrenia have. For example, there is a well-established literature that suggests that individuals with schizophrenia have difficulty following or tracking moving objects with their eyes. Similarly, college students with STPD have difficulty in tracking objects with their eyes. Further, both patients with STPD and patients with schizophrenia have difficulty performing tasks that require focused attention. Finally, recent research using magnetic resonance imaging (MRI), a noninvasive brain imaging technique that uses magnetic waves to study brain structure and activity, suggests that people with schizotypal personality disorder process information similarly to individuals with schizophrenia.

A potential problem in diagnosing schizotypal personality disorders is to mistakenly **pathologize** behaviors that are endorsed by a cultural group. To pathologize a behavior means to call it a symptom of a disorder. For example, some religious groups believe in talking to the dead or believe that people can receive signals from nature. Because of this, a clinician must always consider the context in which the person exhibits his or her beliefs. It is important to ask: Are these beliefs bizarre or extreme within this individual's culture or social group? If odd beliefs are endorsed by a larger group, then the beliefs cannot be considered disordered. A therapist will try to determine whether the client has beliefs that are considered extreme even within his or her subculture. Because peculiar beliefs are only one part of the diagnosis of STPD, however, people who show schizotypal traits and are a part of a culture that endorses paranormal activity can often receive the diagnosis because of their other symptoms.

### REVIEW

Cluster A personality disorders such as paranoid personality disorder (PPD), schizoid personality disorder (SPD), and schizotypal personality disorder (STPD) are characterized by an inability to form or maintain interpersonal relationships. Friendships and romantic relationships are rare for people with Cluster A disorders. Whereas individuals with schizoid or paranoid personality disorder usually are not bothered by their isolation, those with schizotypal personality disorder often feel depressed or anxious about their discomfort in social situations. Finally, it is not uncommon for someone to be diagnosed with more than one Cluster A disorder. For example, a person with paranoid personality disorder might also be diagnosed with schizotypal personality disorder.

# The "Impulsive" Personality Disorders

**I feel like I'm out of control. I just get so angry sometimes, I** don't know what to do. When my boyfriend leaves to go to work, I worry that he isn't going to come back. Sometimes, I feel so empty and numb when I'm alone that I have to do something to feel alive. Usually I just start eating and don't stop until I throw up. I've always felt this way and I'm scared that I always will.

—Anna, a 22-year-old woman diagnosed with borderline personality disorder

People with Cluster B disorders are quite different from those with Cluster A disorders. Whereas individuals with Cluster A disorders tend to be isolated from others, individuals with Cluster B disorders crave attention, admiration, or devotion from other people. They are often emotional, dramatic, and want to be the center of attention. However, because people with Cluster B disorders are unusually demanding or needy, it is difficult for them to maintain interpersonal relationships. There are four Cluster B disorders that we will discuss in this chapter: histrionic, narcissistic, borderline, and antisocial personality disorders.

## HISTRIONIC PERSONALITY DISORDER

Histrionic personality disorder (HPD) is marked by excessive emotionality and extreme attention-seeking behaviors (*histrionic*,

**Figure 3.1** Dramatic public scenes and exaggerated reactions are signs of histrionic personality disorder. © *Holger Winkler/zefa/ CORBIS*

from the Latin word for actor, means theatrical or dramatic). People with HPD need to be center stage (and the only person on stage), and are uncomfortable when they are not. To ensure that they are the center of attention, their interests and conversation will focus on their activities and accomplishments. Seductive or sexually provocative behavior is one way in which someone with HPD will draw attention to him- or herself. Indeed, people with HPD are frequently flirtatious, often inappropriately so. They are often extremely dramatic or flamboyant in ways that make them nearly impossible to ignore. People with HPD will commonly create a scene as a way to guarantee that all eyes are on them. Often, people with HPD enjoy seeing therapists, because the therapist-client relationship provides them with another person's undivided attention.

## CASE STUDY: HISTRIONIC PERSONALITY DISORDER

Since childhood, Elizabeth wanted to participate in activities in which she could be on stage. She competed in beauty pageants, played the piano, studied opera singing and theater, and was a member of a dance troupe. She was very talented and, as a result, every performance she gave was excellent. Still, people always wondered if she was interested in the content of the performance or just the applause that followed.

By the time Elizabeth was 18, she knew hundreds of people. Through her many activities, she had a vast network of acquaintances. However, she rarely maintained contact with people. Sometimes she would get bored with a friend and end the relationship. Other times, her friends got tired of her. During her sophomore year in college, Elizabeth joined a sorority. On the day the new members came to the sorority house, Elizabeth sat in a circle with the other new members. Suddenly, she stated that she had something to say. Instead of beginning to speak, however, she began to sing. The other sorority members were puzzled but complimented her anyway. Over the next three years, Elizabeth's attention-seeking behaviors became commonplace. Eventually, most people grew tired of them.

Even though Elizabeth has had many boyfriends, she has not dated anyone for more than a few months. Her last boyfriend, Anthony, ended their relationship after just three weeks. "At first I thought she was fun to be around. When I took her to a party, I never had to worry about her because she could find something to talk about with anyone. But last weekend, at my friend's place, she started performing a striptease! Out of nowhere! I mean, she didn't take everything off, she still had her bra and underwear on. Still, I didn't know what to make of it. I just left her there. I haven't spoken to her since the party. I don't know if she was on drugs or what!"

After college, Elizabeth began to work as a reporter for a cable television station. She presents stories on people who renovate their homes. Even though she is good at what she does, she wants to be even more famous. She wants more people to know who she is and she will do whatever it takes to get the attention she needs. Lately, she has been considering launching her own site on the Internet that she hopes will be seen by millions of people. The cable station she works for will not allow her to launch her own Web site and still host her home renovation show. She now must decide if she is happy with her small cable show or if she is willing to take the chance for major fame on the Internet.

---

People with HPD often draw attention to themselves with the clothes they wear. They may dress provocatively, or dress up in fancy clothes for everyday activities, or they might actually wear costumes. Physical attractiveness is very important to people with HPD. They want their appearance to be noticed and appreciated by others. They are usually vain and expect to be complimented on how they look. They might even "fish for compliments." Because they are so sensitive about their appearance, they may be deeply hurt by a comment that to another person may seem harmless—for example, if someone says they look tired. They may be excessively disturbed about seeing a bad photograph of themselves.

Even though individuals with histrionic personality disorder tend to be dramatic and emotional, they only experience shallow and shifting emotions. They are very reactive and are prone to throwing temper tantrums. Their speech tends to be vague, impressionistic, and lacking in detail. They might have strong opinions, but when questioned on the reasoning behind those opinions, they will not be able to offer facts to support them. Finally, individuals with HPD have shifting interests. They are highly suggestible and are easily swayed by the opinions of others.

As you might imagine, maintaining a relationship with someone with HPD can be exhausting. These people often alienate their friends with their demands for constant attention. While Anthony enjoyed Elizabeth's outgoing personality at first, her striptease at his friend's party ended their relationship. HPD sufferers' frequently seductive behavior might make it a particular challenge for them to keep their friends of their own sex, because people with HPD might act overly flirtatious or sexually inappropriate with a friend's spouse or partner. Individuals with HPD are quick to make friends, but they have a difficult time keeping them. They might refer to someone they have just met as "my dear, dear friend," then quickly tire of them. Because individuals with HPD are easily bored, they are often quick to drop a friend when they meet someone else they find more interesting.

Like all personality disorders, HPD is rare. Prevalence estimates range from 2 to 3 percent in the general population of the United States. About 10 to 15 percent of patients seeking psychiatric help for mental illness may have HPD. Most individuals diagnosed with HPD are women. There is some speculation that there might be a gender bias in this diagnostic category. That is, the diagnostic criteria might be designed so as to pathologize typical female behaviors. Indeed, there are a number of traits within the diagnostic criteria that are more commonly associated with female rather than male behavior. For instance, women are usually considered more dramatic, vain, and seductive than men. Thus, men with HPD might appear quite different from women with the disorder. Women might be seductive, whereas men might be sexually aggressive. Women might be emotional and dramatic, whereas men might use inappropriate humor. Finally, women might dress provocatively, whereas men might exercise excessively and dress to show off their physique.

## NARCISSISTIC PERSONALITY DISORDER

The key features of narcissistic personality disorder (NPD) are extreme vanity, grandiosity, and a need for admiration. (In Greek mythology, Narcissus was a beautiful youth who fell in love with his own reflection.) People with histrionic personality disorder want attention from other people. People with NPD need not only the attention of others, but their admiration as well. Even though these individuals are concerned with how others view them, they are remarkably self-centered. That is, they lack empathy for the thoughts and concerns of others. In essence, people with NPD believe that they are unique and deserve special treatment.

### CASE STUDY: NARCISSISTIC PERSONALITY DISORDER

Violet is a housewife who lives in the New England countryside. Her husband, Mark, is a doctor who has a small practice in their town. They have two children, both of whom are in college. Violet is active in several philanthropic organizations and is on the board of the botanical garden in the next town. She has few friends and believes that this is because most people envy her. Mark knows that this is not true and has taken Violet to a therapist to help figure out the reason for her interpersonal problems.

When Violet went to her first appointment with the therapist, her first question was, "Where did you train?" Violet was skeptical when she learned that the therapist is a licensed clinical social worker, and later told Mark that she would prefer to speak with someone with a medical degree, or at the very least, a doctorate. This is common behavior for Violet. When Mark first met her, he was studying medicine at Harvard and she was a student at another college in Boston. She knew she wanted to marry a "Harvard man" and was only willing to date men who were students at Harvard. Initially, Mark felt special because Violet liked him. She constantly told him how smart and talented he was and how much she expected of him. Recently he has begun to feel that he is a disappointment to her because she frequently tells him that he should have made more of a name for himself by working in a big-city hospital.

Most of the women with whom Violet has volunteered dislike her. When she worked for the town library, Violet offended the librarian by telling her that she didn't know how to do her job. When Violet worked for a hospice, two nurses quit rather than continue working with her after she demanded to review each patient's chart at the end of the day. Now she is having similar problems at the botanical garden. In her role as board member, she calls for weekly meetings, which she leads. She asks the volunteers to report on their progress with their activities. She evaluates everyone's progress, and, if she finds it lacking, she voices her disapproval. Because of the way

**Figure 3.2** People with narcissistic personality disorder often don't realize how unpleasant they seem to those around them. © *Tim Garcha/zefa/CORBIS*

she treats people, three of the five other board members have left and donations have dropped.

Violet seems to be unaware of how her behavior affects others. She tells Mark that people have left the board of the botanical garden because they realize they are unable to keep up with Violet's high standards. Mark and Violet are rarely invited to social events but Violet dismisses this as a result of people's envy. She says, "We remind them of everything they don't have. Besides, people like us shouldn't be expected to socialize with just anybody!"

Mark has a lot of friends and would like to be able to see more of them. As it is, he goes out for a weekly poker game but rarely sees his friends outside of this one night a week. He tries to tell Violet that her snobbish behavior is making him unhappy and is the cause of their social isolation, but she is dismissive. Mark's last hope was to go for marital counseling. Now that Violet has decided that she thinks the therapist isn't good enough for them, he doesn't know what he will do.

Violet believes and acts as though she is superior to others. People with narcissistic personality disorder usually alienate others with their inflated self-esteem, excessive bragging, and exaggeration of their abilities. They might overestimate their own talents, while underestimating the talents of others. Narcissists are often consumed with fantasies of great fame, success, or power. They might also be preoccupied with dreams of ideal beauty or romantic love. Because they believe they are unique, people with NPD might compare themselves favorably to famous or privileged people. Further, they are often only interested in associating with accomplished people, demanding to see the top doctor when they need to have a medical checkup. Even though the therapist came highly recommended, Violet was unhappy when she learned that the therapist had a master's degree rather than a doctorate. Violet's sense of superiority makes her believe that she can only be understood by similarly special people.

---

Individuals with NPD rarely see problems with their behavior. Indeed, Violet cannot see that her offensive behavior is the reason she has few friends. Entitlement is a key feature of narcissistic personality disorder. People with NPD often expect to be catered to and are angry and confused when this does not happen. If someone with NPD is a manager or in a position of power at work, she is often unpopular with her employees. She may exploit her employees to further her own career. Relationships are usually superficial and difficult for people with NPD. Usually, a narcissist will only form friendships or romantic relationships if the other person seems likely to enhance her self-esteem or help her in some way. The narcissist's self-centeredness means that she lacks an appreciation for other people's points of view. It is difficult for her to understand that other people might have their own thoughts and feelings and that the narcissist's well-being is not the most important thing to everyone else. Seth Rosenthal at Harvard University believes that the narcissist's grandiose self-image protects him from low self-esteem.

Although you might be able to think of someone you know who is extremely vain, clinical narcissistic personality disorder is rare and affects less than 1 percent of the population of the United States. Men are more likely than women to develop this disorder, and they rarely seek treatment for their problems. In truth, most narcissists can't imagine they have any problems at all! Recall that Violet believed that the envy of other people was the reason she had few social relationships. People with NPD are most likely to be brought to therapy by an employer, spouse, or family member.

## BORDERLINE PERSONALITY DISORDER

The term *borderline* has a long and confusing history. Many years ago, *borderline* referred to a condition that was thought to exist on the "border" between **psychotic** and **neurotic** states. This meant that individuals with borderline disorders were experiencing a sort of mild schizophrenia. Psychologists no longer use the term *borderline* in the same way. In fact, what used to be thought of as *borderline* is now considered to be schizotypal personality disorder (see Chapter 2). Today, borderline personality disorder (BPD) is the most common personality disorder encountered by clinicians. It is marked primarily by instability of moods, self-image, and interpersonal relationships. Someone with BPD wants close and meaningful relationships. Unfortunately, their unpredictable behavior can push others away. Because someone with BPD is often moody, needy, and demanding, they can be very difficult friends or partners.

**CASE STUDY: BORDERLINE PERSONALITY DISORDER**

Lynne is a 30-year-old nurse who was brought to the hospital after her most recent suicide attempt. Her family has all but given up on her, and no one comes to visit her in the hospital anymore. Her mother says that this is the eleventh time that Lynne has been taken to the hospital, this time for swallowing a bottle of Tylenol®. "This wasn't for real," her mother tells the doctor. "If it was serious, she would have taken the prescription pain killers like she did last time."

Lynne has been married twice and divorced once. Her second husband left her and has not contacted her for six months. Even though she is technically married, she has a new boyfriend, Kevin, whom she met six weeks ago through an Internet dating site. Kevin left to go camping with some friends, which may have triggered this most recent suicide attempt. Lynne has no way to contact Kevin, since he doesn't have cell phone reception where he is camping. She is angry and feels isolated and believes she has no way of conveying her loneliness.

"I have always felt alone and empty," Lynne tells her therapist. "As long as I can remember. I kept trying different things to find myself, but all I find is disappointment. I think I'll be happy once I meet my soul mate. So far, I haven't had much luck, but I think Kevin could be the one. Well, he could have been, if he hadn't been so selfish to just take off with his friends with no concern for my feelings."

Lynne reports a pattern of relationship failures in which every man she has dated has disappointed her. Each relationship begins as a great romance, and then is filled with arguments that sometimes turn physical. Several times in each relationship, Lynne has either started cutting herself or has attempted suicide. Every man she has dated has visited her in the hospital, and that's when she feels the most secure.

Because of her frequent depression and suicide attempts, it took Lynne nine years to finish nursing school. She also dropped out of school three times to try different careers. Once she joined a band as a singer and traveled around the southwestern United States playing in small bars. Another time, she decided she wanted to be a teacher and began working at a preschool. When that no longer interested her, she decided to take up painting. After she received some lukewarm feedback on some of her work, she decided that the art teacher didn't like her and dropped out of the class. After several years of floating from job to job, she became a nurse at a local hospital. Unfortunately, it has been difficult to keep a steady job at a hospital with all of the "mental health days" she takes. If she doesn't get out of the psychiatric hospital soon, she will most likely lose her current job.

---

**Emotional dysregulation**, or problems maintaining stable and appropriate mood states, is often considered a hallmark of BPD. As with Lynne, many people with BPD frequently show up at hospital emergency rooms because they feel out of control, hopeless, and depressed. The extreme reactivity of mood in BPD may cause some of these individuals to throw temper tantrums or have tremendous difficulty controlling their anger.

Someone with BPD might react violently to what would only be mildly irritating to someone else. Chronic anxiety and depression are common with BPD. Because BPD sufferers are highly reactive to things that happen around them, they may become extremely anxious, angry, or depressed because of a minor interpersonal problem or social irritant. For example, someone with BPD might become extremely angry if a friend answers a call on her cell phone while they are meeting for coffee. As with other personality disorders, extreme stress can cause minor psychotic symptoms. Thus, people with BPD might become paranoid or dissociate temporarily when overwhelmed at home or at work. **Dissociation** is a process in which thoughts or memories are cut off from consciousness. When someone dissociates (their mind splits consciousness), they might feel as though they are watching themselves from afar or having an "out-of-body" experience. **Impulsivity**, or acting without thinking about the consequences, coupled with the extreme moodiness of people with BPD, may lead them to engage in dangerous and harmful activities such as binge eating, sexual promiscuity, alcohol and drug abuse, reckless driving, gambling, and self-mutilation.

A history of extremely stormy and unstable relationships is one characteristic of borderline personality disorder. Lynne recalls that all of her relationships have been passionate, filled with intense feelings of love and hate. Similarly, individuals with BPD often engage in "all-or-nothing" thinking, viewing people as either all good or all bad. For example, a boyfriend might be seen as a wonderful, generous caregiver. However, after the boyfriend comes home half an hour late one night, he might be viewed as evil and cruel. Someone without BPD is usually able to understand that even though her boyfriend was late, he can still be a kind and loving person. Someone with BPD might not be able to understand that making a small mistake (being late one time) does not mean that her boyfriend is all bad. When a

BPD patient goes from viewing someone as kind and good to viewing them as evil and bad it is called "**splitting**."

Dealing with the drama and instability of someone with BPD is a challenge. It is not uncommon for their partners to try to leave the relationship. Unfortunately, ending a relationship with someone with BPD is not so easy. An intense fear of rejection or abandonment may cause these individuals to engage in frantic and desperate acts to get attention and keep a loved one close to them. For example, Lynne recalls that she used suicide attempts or self-mutilating behaviors (such as cutting or burning herself without suicidal intent) to prevent her partner from leaving. Indeed, self-mutilation is one of the most characteristic signs of BPD. Some individuals with BPD report that harming themselves gives them relief from anxiety or depression or makes them feel "real." Others may attempt self-mutilation to prevent separation from a loved one or a therapist. Remember that self-mutilation is different from repeated attempts to commit suicide. Self-mutilation is designed only to inflict harm and not be life-threatening. An example of self-mutilation is carving the initials of a loved one into the skin. Although this is painful and violent, it is not lethal. A suicide attempt, such as taking an overdose of medication, is not necessarily painful but can result in death. Many individuals with BPD attempt suicide, often multiple times. About 8 percent of suicide attempts end in death, and so every attempt must be taken seriously.

Finally, many individuals with BPD report feeling "empty" inside, which might come from loneliness or the person's sense that she doesn't know who she is. These feelings are thought to accompany an intolerance of being alone, or may be associated with an unstable sense of self. Indeed, individuals with BPD often report a shifting sense of who they are. They might experiment with different career paths (as we saw with Lynne) or religious beliefs in order to feel more grounded in their identity. In their efforts to discover just where they belong, it is not uncommon for them to find entirely new groups of friends. In sum, these people have a difficult time figuring out who they are and may take drastic means to define their individuality. They may do this by getting several tattoos or body piercings, joining a new group or club, or changing careers.

Borderline personality disorder is a significant public health concern. Recent estimates suggest that at any given time, 10 to 20 percent of all psychiatric patients have the disorder. Some 75 percent of individuals with BPD are female, although there is some speculation that the diagnosis, like histrionic personality disorder, may be gender-biased. In order for the criteria to be biased, diagnostic symptoms must be more likely to be expressed by women. Another explanation for the reported predominance is that women are much more likely to seek treatment, and most prevalence estimates come from clinical samples. According to this explanation, men are just as likely to exhibit symptoms of BPD but are much less likely to see a therapist. More research is needed to clarify how men and women with BPD differ as well as what features they share.

## ANTISOCIAL PERSONALITY DISORDER

As with borderline personality disorder, the history of the diagnosis of **antisocial personality disorder (ASPD)** is fairly long and complex. You may have heard the terms *sociopath* and *psychopath*, which are used to refer to individuals who behave violently, aggressively, and selfishly. The popular media often apply these labels to serial killers, such as Ted Bundy. Indeed, the features of the "psychopath" and "sociopath" are similar to current descriptions of ASPD.

Perhaps the most extensively studied personality disorder, antisocial personality disorder (ASPD) is characterized by a persistent and pervasive disregard for and violation of the rights of others. Unique to ASPD is the requirement that the clinician consider the person's behavior in childhood (before the age of 15). In fact, to receive the diagnosis of ASPD, a person must display at least some symptoms of **conduct disorder**, a disorder of childhood in which children engage in repeatedly aggressive or destructive behavior. Examples of such behavior include: (1) aggression toward people and/or animals, (2) destruction of property, (3) deceitfulness or theft, and (4) serious violation of rules. In adulthood, someone who has ASPD usually continues to engage in behaviors that harm others, and he is indifferent to how his behavior affects other people.

### CASE STUDY: ANTISOCIAL PERSONALITY DISORDER

Rick is a 30-year-old father of two children who is having significant marital problems. Rick is married to Valerie. They met in high school and started dating in their freshman year. Valerie fell head-over-heels in love with Rick. He was good-looking, a star athlete, and president of his senior class. She thought he was very charming, and also thought that there was something dangerous and exciting about him. Indeed, Rick could be physically aggressive and turn very violent. Sometimes he got into fights after football games. On at least one occasion, he injured another boy so badly that the boy had to go to the hospital. Apparently, Rick has always been violent. One of his friends told Valerie that when they were 10, Rick beat a small cat to death and buried it in his backyard. Even so, Valerie thought he was powerful and she felt special because he chose her. They started dating in high school, continued dating through college, and married shortly after graduation. Now, at age 30, they have two children and Valerie is having second thoughts about their marriage.

Rick is away from home a lot—for work, he claims. However, last week a woman called their house looking for him. When Valerie introduced herself as his wife, the other woman told her that she was his fiancée. Valerie was shocked and started asking people in her community about her husband. To her amazement, she learned that Rick had dated several other women since they got married.

Learning about Rick's infidelity has made Valerie less tolerant of some of his other questionable behaviors. Rick has received several speeding tickets and one arrest for drunk driving. His license is currently suspended, but he continues to drive anyway. He often stays out late playing poker with friends. On a few occasions, he has taken spontaneous weekend trips to Las Vegas and lost money—a lot more money than they can afford. Last month, he gambled away the money for their mortgage payment and told Valerie to ask her parents for a loan. Even though they have borrowed thousands of dollars from her parents in recent years, there is no evidence that Rick has any intention of paying them back.

Valerie loves her husband. He is handsome and he has a great sense of humor. However, she is tired of waiting around for him to show up when it suits him. She also doesn't know what to tell her sons, who rarely see their father. Rick has been going to see a therapist with Valerie, but has little interest in participating in the sessions. He denies the affairs he has had, even when Valerie presents proof, and, when she confronts him with his gambling debts, he insists that he has lost only a few hundred dollars. Valerie is hurt and confused.

---

Most of the features of antisocial personality disorder are behaviors one can observe, rather than thoughts or feelings. These behaviors usually indicate a pattern of being indifferent to the interests of others. Someone with ASPD might show a consistent failure to obey the law and may engage in such acts as destruction of property, harassing others, or theft. Like Rick, these individuals are usually deceitful and manipulative and will lie or charm others to obtain money, power, or sex. Lying is a common trait of ASPD, and affected individuals can tell lies with ease. Like people with BPD, individuals with ASPD are impulsive and usually fail to plan ahead. They make decisions on the spur of the moment and may decide to leave one job without having another. As a result, they often report long periods of time without regular employment. As parents, they may be extremely irresponsible, leaving their family on the spur of the moment without arranging for financial support or supervision for their children. Rick found the time to play poker with his friends but rarely came home when he said he would.

In adulthood as well as in childhood, aggressive behavior is characteristic of ASPD. Often irritable and aggressive, ASPD sufferers may engage in physical fights. Their aggression may extend to family members, and people with ASPD frequently commit acts of domestic violence. In addition to physical aggression, people with ASPD display a reckless disregard for their own safety and that of others and may engage in risky behaviors, such as substance abuse or reckless driving.

Despite all the harm these individuals may cause, they usually do not feel any remorse or guilt. People with ASPD are often cynical, callous, arrogant, and cocky. Some individuals with ASPD are extremely intelligent and charming. The combination of charm, recklessness, and indifference to others can create an extremely manipulative and potentially dangerous person.

Antisocial personality disorder is three times more common in males than in females. Within the general population of the United States, about 3 percent of males have ASPD. Within clinical settings, the estimate rises to as much as 30 percent. In prison settings, the rates of ASPD are even higher. ASPD appears to be more common in males of low socioeconomic

# Ted Bundy: A Psychopath in Action

Ted Bundy is perhaps the best example of antisocial personality disorder in the extreme. A handsome and charming man, Bundy was convicted and sentenced to death for the brutal murder of more than 20 women. In fact, even though he confessed to at least 28 murders, some experts suspect that he is guilty of murdering more than 30 women. While he was in prison awaiting execution, Bundy was the subject of study as an example of a "psychopath."

A shy, quiet child, Bundy was often the target of teasing and bullying. Although he reported feeling unpopular in junior high and high school, early descriptions reveal that he was a good student, was well-dressed, and had good manners. Bundy obtained a high grade point average in college where he studied psychology. Eventually, he became interested in politics and was active in the Republican Party. He applied to law school and worked as a rape counselor in Seattle, Washington.

Bundy used his good looks and charm to get close to his victims. With an artificial cast on his arm or leg, he approached women and asked for help carrying something to his car. His victims, usually young, pretty girls with long, dark hair parted in the middle, were dragged into his car, handcuffed, sexually assaulted, and eventually murdered. After a lengthy police search, Bundy was apprehended, escaped, and committed more serial murders before he was caught for good.

He maintained his innocence, claiming that his prosecution was due in large part to the media's eagerness to see him prosecuted. Despite ample evidence confirming his guilt, Bundy brazenly claimed that he was the victim. Prior to his execution in 1989 in Florida, he confessed to at least 28 murders. Like most people with antisocial personality disorder, Ted Bundy showed no remorse for his behavior.

status. When assessing ASPD, it is crucial to consider the motive for unlawful behavior. For example, stealing to provide food for one's children should not be considered evidence of ASPD. If unlawful behavior occurs only as a part of a survival strategy, it is not likely to be an antisocial act.

## REVIEW

Cluster B personality disorders are characterized by dramatic, emotional, and attention-seeking behaviors. People with these disorders tend to be extremely sensitive and reactive to interpersonal events. Although people with Cluster B disorders want to be in relationships, their motives for relationships are usually selfish. As a result, their relationships tend to be volatile and unstable. Finally, it is common for Cluster B personality disorders to occur in the same person at the same time. For example, someone with antisocial or borderline personality disorder might have characteristics of narcissistic or histrionic personality disorder.

# The "Anxious" Personality Disorders

**The worst part of my day is lunchtime. When I'm at work, I'm** alone at my desk. But at lunch, I have to go to the cafeteria and sit with other people. My coworkers try to talk to me, they ask questions and seem interested in me. But I'm just so boring. I never know what to say and worry that I'm going to offend somebody. My heart starts racing at 11:45 because I know that in 15 minutes I have to start my walk downstairs. After lunch I worry about what I said and who I may have upset. I wish I could be funny and interesting. I wish I was normal.

> —Abigail, a 33-year-old woman diagnosed
> with avoidant personality disorder.

Someone with "anxious" personality disorders is often tense, uptight, and worried. Fearful by nature, she often avoids situations in which she does not know what to expect. Like people with the "odd" personality disorders, those with "anxious" personality disorders are uncomfortable around most other people. However, these groups differ in a significant way. People with "odd" personality disorders tend to avoid other people because they worry that others might be out to get them or might harm them in some way. On the other hand, people with "anxious" personality disorders *want* to have relationships, but are often unable to relax and feel comfortable in the company of others. The three disorders we will discuss in this chapter are avoidant

personality disorder, dependent personality disorder, and obsessive-compulsive personality disorder.

## AVOIDANT PERSONALITY DISORDER

People with **avoidant personality disorder (APD)** shy away from
other people because they are afraid of being criticized or
embarrassed, or worry that they will appear foolish. Usually,
someone with APD is very concerned that if he is criticized, he
will blush or cry in front of other people. He often feels inadequate, which makes him inhibited in social situations. People
with APD might believe they are so unappealing that they think
that no one would want to know them or be friends with them.
They will usually refuse to be in a relationship unless they are
sure that the other person will like and accept them. To make
sure that others like them, they are often "eager to please."
Ironically, people with APD often behave in a way that confirms
their negative self-image. They are so sensitive to criticism that
they often misinterpret innocent comments as negative or critical. When they interact with other people, they may act fearful
or tense, and make mistakes, which often prompts others to
tease or criticize them.

### CASE STUDY: AVOIDANT PERSONALITY DISORDER

Michele, a 25-year-old garden center employee, has lived a
relatively isolated life. Although she was a cheerful and generally uninhibited child, during her teen years she became
extremely anxious and shy. Her performance in school began
to slip when she was assigned to a group project in history
class. To avoid having to work with the other students, she
skipped class and eventually failed the course. Although she is
very bright, Michele has been unable to finish school because
she is so uncomfortable in the classroom setting. She prefers
to be alone, where she enjoys reading and painting with

watercolors. She will not speak in class and she doesn't like to work with other students. After she graduated from high school, she took a job working with plants in a garden center and has kept the same job for seven years.

Michele has one friend, May, whom she has known for 10 years. May is a strong, opinionated person, and she is often mean and critical to Michele. Michele wants to make other friends, but she feels so unattractive and boring that no one would want to be friends with her. Because of her sense of inferiority, Michele spends most of her free time at home with her parents or with May.

Michele is very good at her job. She is very knowledgeable about plants and how to care for them. On the few occasions when she has come out of the nursery and onto the sales floor, she has done a great job helping customers. However, when she was required to help out in sales, she became extremely nervous. She is consumed with thoughts that she's going to make a mistake and be criticized by a customer, and she worries that she will embarrass herself by saying something stupid. Although Michele's boss would like her to take a position as assistant manager, Michele is not interested in the promotion. Although she is highly qualified for the job, the position would require too much socializing with new people. "Besides," Michele thinks, "I would probably mess up anyway."

---

Because they are so uncomfortable around other people, people with APD usually have very few or no close friends other than someone in their immediate family. Michele is willing to stay in an unhealthy friendship with May because she believes she isn't appealing enough to make friends with other people. APD sufferers are usually distant or restrained in romantic relationships because they are afraid of being made fun of or ashamed if they reveal too much about themselves: other people would see their weaknesses and inadequacies. They also avoid jobs where socializing is required.

People with APD rarely seek help from a therapist because they are so uncomfortable talking to other people. Because they avoid therapy, too, it is difficult to estimate the prevalence of avoidant personality disorder. Research suggests that less than 1 percent of the population of the United States has APD. This estimate rises to 10 percent of patients receiving psychiatric treatment, many of whom may already be undergoing treatment for other mental health concerns such as depression.

Avoidant personality disorder might sound a lot like schizoid personality disorder, since people with both kinds of disorders are "loners," but they are different in at least one crucial way. Whereas an "avoider" is isolated because of hypersensitivity to criticism, shyness, and low self-esteem, someone with schizoid personality disorder is cold and indifferent to criticism.

## DEPENDENT PERSONALITY DISORDER

People with dependent personality disorder (DPD) doubt their ability to take care of themselves, which leads to clinging, submissive behavior. Being abandoned or separated from a caregiver causes them extreme distress, so they will typically do whatever they have to do to keep others close to them. Someone with DPD has difficulty making everyday decisions, starting projects, and expressing her own opinions. Unfortunately, she has such an extreme need to obtain and keep the support of others that she's often willing to compromise her own interests in order to avoid being alone. *Dependent personality disorder is the most frequently encountered personality disorder in mental health clinics.*

**CASE STUDY: DEPENDENT PERSONALITY DISORDER**

Theresa is a 30-year-old administrative assistant for a large publishing company. She has worked for the company for three months and, in many ways, her boss, Kate, is very impressed with her work. Theresa is always punctual, detail-oriented, and conscientious. She keeps the office kitchen immaculate and always has a fresh pot of coffee prepared. She is the first person to get to the office in the morning and the last person to leave at night. One morning, after a bad rainstorm, some of the pipes backed up and the sink overflowed. Theresa cleaned up the mess all alone without being asked. However, despite her willingness to handle unpleasant tasks, Theresa needs a lot of supervision. Whenever she is given a task to complete, she e-mails Kate a long list of questions that range from what font to use to type a letter to how best to organize a set of files. Kate finds that sometimes, giving a letter to Theresa to type takes longer than doing it herself! Kate wants Theresa to talk to the company therapist and have a mental health evaluation.

Theresa grew up in a small town in the Midwest and is the middle child with two brothers. Her father died when she was very young and her mother was forced to move the family in with her parents. Her grandmother was very domineering, always telling Theresa what to do and how to do it. Every night, Theresa would give her homework to her grandmother to review and, often, her grandmother would completely redo it. When she graduated from high school, Theresa enrolled at a community college. She wanted to move to a city an hour away from their home but her grandmother told her, "You'll never make it. You should just stay home with us. You're too young and immature to take care of yourself!" Theresa grew frustrated at being at home with her family. She was tired of being bossed around by her grandmother, and was angry with her mother, who rarely intervened on her behalf. At the age of 20, Theresa married Jordan, her Spanish teacher. Jordan was 13 years her senior, but by all accounts, he was a kind man and a good provider.

Even though Theresa's friends like Jordan, they do not think that he and Theresa have a healthy marriage. He makes all the decisions in the household. They usually socialize with his family, his friends, and participate in activities that he chooses. When she is alone, she will often call Jordan and ask his advice on where to eat or where to buy groceries. Theresa says that she likes the same things Jordan does, but her friends know this is not true. She has never told Jordan what she thinks or feels because she wants to keep him happy and keep him near her. Recently, she has become nervous because Jordan is talking about starting a family. She is afraid that Jordan will find out that she isn't capable of raising a child. She doesn't want to disappoint him, but she questions her ability to be a mother.

---

Luckily for Theresa, her husband is kind and supportive. Often, people with dependent personality disorder find themselves in physically or emotionally abusive relationships. Because they feel so incapable of taking care of themselves, they will choose to remain in an unpleasant situation rather than live on their own. They often ask a lot from their friends and family. They need excessive advice before making even an ordinary, everyday decision (such as what to order in a restaurant or what to wear). Just as Theresa asked her boss for opinions on tiny details of a task, people with DPD will have trouble starting projects or completing them independently. They lack the confidence that they will be able to complete a task to the satisfaction of others. To make sure that others will like them, someone

**Figure 4.1** Extreme perfectionist expectations can be part of obsessive-compulsive personality disorder. © *PushPictures/CORBIS*

with DPD is willing to do even unpleasant things. When Theresa cleaned up the mess from the backed-up sink, she was trying to make herself useful and hoping others would see her as someone they wanted to have around. If people with DPD are separated from a caregiver, they will quickly find someone else to provide for them. These people are never alone for long.

### OBSESSIVE-COMPULSIVE PERSONALITY DISORDER

Perfectionism and rigidity are the principal characteristics of obsessive-compulsive personality disorder (OCPD). The obsessive-compulsive personality is overly concerned with organization, rules, and order. Their perfectionism often prevents them from finishing projects, since they are rarely convinced that a project is good enough to be considered "finished." These people have trouble "seeing the forest for the trees," because they are focused on details rather than the whole picture. Often, people with OCPD are considered workaholics. They rarely take vacations and can usually be found focused on some project or another. OCPD should not be confused with obsessive-compulsive disorder (OCD). Obsessive-compulsive disorder (without the word *personality* in the term) is an illness in which an individual is bothered by either persistent, uncontrollable thoughts or behaviors that they are compelled to repeat again and again. It is a cyclical disorder, which means that the symptoms come and go. Personality traits typical of obsessive-compulsive *personality* disorder, on the other hand, are stable and long-lasting and are seen in nearly all cases.

### CASE STUDY: OBSESSIVE-COMPULSIVE DISORDER

Sarah is a writer for a small newspaper. This is her first job since college and she wants to keep it. She has aspirations of becoming a top journalist someday, perhaps winning a Pulitzer Prize. However, she is on the verge of losing her job because she missed a series of deadlines.

Always considered a "neat freak," Sarah spends a lot of time cleaning and organizing her cubicle at work. Before she can begin writing an article, her desk must be in order and all her notes in place. Even if she is reporting on a small civic celebration, a story that will take up only a tiny amount of space in the newspaper, Sarah will construct a detailed outline, including everything she knows about the subject. Her outlines are so detailed that they often exceed the amount of space that will be allotted to the story in the paper by five times. But to Sarah the outline is an important part of writing. She says it helps her organize her thoughts. Unfortunately, when her article is due, she is usually still working on the outline.

Sarah works very hard at her job. She is in the office first thing in the morning and often stays until after 9:00 P.M. Her editor is generally happy with her writing, but she has to be more prompt in submitting her finished articles. (Newspapers live or die by deadlines.) More than once, her tardiness has left an awkward space in the paper that had to be filled with an advertisement or a piece from the Associated Press. The editor has asked Sarah to be more conscious of deadlines, but Sarah is unable to change her routine.

Other people in the office do not like to work with Sarah. When she works in a group, she is reluctant to let anyone else contribute much to the project. Ever the perfectionist, Sarah believes her way is the right way and doesn't think other people will do a good job. She obsessively does her own research even though she has an assistant who is supposed to do that for her. She doesn't ask for help because she believes that she "will have to do the work herself anyway, so why not start right the first time?" All this work leaves Sarah very little time for a social life. Sarah has never had a date, rarely goes anywhere other than work, and has no hobbies. She has not taken a vacation since she was in junior high, when her parents refused to leave her at home alone. In college, she used her vacation time to get a head start on the next semester's reading list and now she is unwilling to leave the office. Her editor is concerned about her and feels that he might just have to let her go.

Although Sarah is a perfectionist, a hard worker with high aspirations, her obsession with details and organization makes it difficult for her to complete tasks. She has problems finishing projects because she gets sidetracked by the details. Planning is very important. These people will plan everything, even every minute of their spare time. However, although they are good planners, they often have problems prioritizing and end up missing deadlines. People with obsessive-compulsive personality disorder are often thrifty or stingy. They have a tough time throwing things away, even useless things that are worn out and have no sentimental value. In fact, their homes can become crowded with old newspapers, used yogurt containers (you never know when you might need one!), broken appliances, etc., and they are often considered "pack rats." Their hoarding may get so bad that others will complain about the mess. People with OCPD may keep useless things around or hoard money in an attempt to be prepared for future catastrophes. Even if they have plenty of money, they may be excessively miserly.

## The Downside of Perfectionism

Many people think of perfectionism as a desirable trait, for perfectionists are typically hard workers, responsible and determined, and with an eye for detail. Their high standards ensure that they achieve goals that may appear out of reach to other people. However, the problem with perfectionism is that the drive to achieve can become all-consuming and has been associated with at least two forms of mental illness: (1) anorexia nervosa, an eating disorder in which individuals (usually young women) go to extreme lengths to lose weight, and (2) obsessive-compulsive personality disorder, a personality disorder marked by a rigidity and stubbornness. In addition, perfectionism has been associated with a potentially deadly physical condition— coronary heart disease, which occurs when arteries that supply blood to the heart become partially blocked. Research suggests some qualities of perfectionism, such as frequent frustration, may increase the risk of developing coronary heart disease.

People with OCPD are very critical of themselves and others. Just as Sarah couldn't work with other people in her office, most OCPD sufferers are unwilling to delegate tasks or have others help them. They have difficulty acknowledging others' opinions or points of view and believe that everything must be done "their way." As you might imagine, friends or family members often find them rigid, stubborn, and difficult. People with obsessive-compulsive personality disorder are often deferential to authority and highly moralistic. They may refuse to bend the rules even in a case when a rule is clearly unreasonable. For example, someone with OCPD might tell you that they have never driven faster than the speed limit. Whereas most people

In 1948, researchers in Framingham, Massachusetts, began an ambitious project. They recruited thousands of participants in order to identify factors that contribute to the development of cardiovascular disease. Researchers followed study participants throughout their lives, focusing on various aspects of the participant's health and lifestyle. The Framingham Heart Study revealed very convincing data about the relationship between Type A personality traits and coronary heart disease. Researchers found that participants who were identified as Type A personalities were twice as likely to develop coronary heart disease. Over the last 30 years, several more studies have examined this correlation. In fact, researchers have revealed certain Type A qualities that may be more associated with coronary heart disease than others. It appears hostility is the component of Type A personality that is most likely to contribute to coronary heart disease.

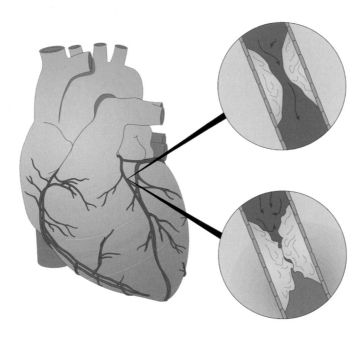

**Figure 4.2** Having a type A personality can contribute to increased risk for coronary artery disease, in which fatty plaques clog the arteries and block the flow of blood from the heart. © *Peter Gardiner/ Photo Researchers, Inc.*

will acknowledge that there have been occasions when they have exceeded the speed limit, someone with OCPD might consider even mild speeding a serious offense.

You may have heard of "type A" personalities—people who are extremely focused and driven. People with OCPD may also be considered "type A," but their inability to see the "big picture" sometimes hurts them at work and at home. They can be very difficult to work for, because their high personal standards may be impossible to satisfy. Further, they make challenging spouses because they are rarely spontaneous or able to relax.

Obsessive-compulsive personality disorder appears to be twice as common in males as in females. The disorder appears in about 1 in 100 people in the general population of the United States and in about 3 to 10 percent of people who seek help at mental health clinics.

### REVIEW

People with "anxious" personality disorders are often tense, uptight, and worried. They tend to be so concerned with how they appear to other people that they cannot relax at work or in a social situation. Although "anxious" personality disorders share several qualities with anxiety disorders in general, recall that personality disorders are pervasive and persistent. That is, whereas someone with an anxiety disorder might have occasional episodes of anxiety or have anxiety only in certain situations, someone with an "anxious" personality disorder is anxious and experiencing symptoms of the disorder most of the time in most or all situations.

# 5 Causes of Personality Disorders

**Personality disorders begin in childhood and continue into** adulthood. For this reason, it is often difficult to determine exactly when the disorder began. Most likely, personality disorders emerge slowly over a period of several years. It is not uncommon for personality disorders to go untreated for a long time, because these behaviors become so much a part of the person's identity that it is difficult for him or her to realize that something is wrong. So, what causes personality disorders to develop? Do they run in families? Are they the result of biological influences? Are they caused by family or social environment? Do traumatic events play a role in the development of personality disorders? In fact, all of these may be possible. It appears that personality disorders arise from a combination of factors that may be genetic, biological, and environmental. The goal of clinician-researchers is to take a biopsychosocial perspective in understanding mental disorders. This means that they strive to understand which biological, psychological, and social influences combine to create a personality disorder. In this chapter, we will discuss what current research tells us about the causes of personality disorders. Because so many elements may be involved, identifying the exact cause of a personality disorder is not a simple matter, but researchers are steadily developing a better understanding of the relevant factors.

## CHALLENGES IN STUDYING THE CAUSES OF PERSONALITY DISORDERS

Psychological research is challenging, particularly when the topic is personality disorders. There are several reasons for this. Personality disorders are a fairly new category of psychological disorders. Personality disorders were first defined in 1980 in the third edition of the *Diagnostic and Statistical Manual of Mental Disorders* (DSM), the primary reference work used by mental health professionals (mentioned in Chapter 1). Thus, these disorders have been officially recognized for only around 25 years.

There is also a great deal of **diagnostic comorbidity** in personality disorders. This means that people who have one personality disorder are highly likely to have at least one more. In fact, a study by Thomas Widiger and colleagues at the University of Kentucky found that 85 percent of patients who had a personality disorder actually had more than one.[3] Finally, someone with a personality disorder often has another mental disorder, such as a mood or anxiety disorder, for example, major depressive disorder or panic disorder. Having multiple diagnoses makes it particularly difficult to isolate one disorder to study its origins.

## BIOLOGICAL INFLUENCES

Genes are the building blocks of human beings. Every human characteristic, from the color of your hair to your preference for sweet or savory foods, may have its origin in your genetic makeup. There are ample data to suggest that personality traits are **heritable**, or passed down from one generation to the next. You have probably have observed this phenomenon in your own life. Perhaps your mother tells you that you have your father's temper or your grandmother's sense of humor. These qualities are at least partly determined by your genetic makeup. Often it is possible to trace one's personality back to childhood.

For example, your mother might tell you that you have always been gregarious and outgoing (or, perhaps, you have always been both outgoing and private, needing time to yourself to read, make things, etc.). Indeed, we may observe a hint of their future adult personality in young children. The foundation of adult personality, as it is observed in infants, is called temperament.

## TEMPERAMENT

An infant's "temperament" is the way the infant responds to environmental stimuli.[4] Babies differ in how they respond to various situations. For example, some infants are startled by bright light or loud noises, while others are less affected by these kinds of sensory stimuli. Some infants cling to their mothers, whereas others seem comfortable with a wide variety of caregivers. By observing the way infants respond to stimuli in their environments, researchers can predict how they might respond to stimuli in adulthood. In fact, some researchers believe that temperament in infancy may be related to personality as described in the Five-Factor Model we saw in Chapter 1(the five traits are extroversion, agreeableness, conscientiousness, emotional stability, and openness to experience). For example, infants who are often fearful or irritable may be anxious or fearful as adults, or considered highly **neurotic**. Alternatively, infants who are happy and energetic may be highly **extroverted** and relaxed as adults.

Given that temperament is the foundation of normal adult personality, it is not surprising that temperament might predict psychopathology in adulthood. Kagan and his colleagues[5] at Harvard University have found that infants who are **behaviorally inhibited**, or significantly fearful, are more likely to develop anxiety disorders as children and as adults. Alternatively, children who show little fear of threats, or are **behaviorally uninhibited**, might have difficulty learning appropriate behavior and have been shown to exhibit more aggressive and delinquent behavior when observed by researchers at age 13.[6] So far, there are few existing data that directly and specifically link temperament to the development of personality disorders. Future research will no doubt address this question.

### DO PERSONALITY DISORDERS RUN IN FAMILIES?

We have established that certain personality traits may be heritable, or passed down from one generation to the next. But is the same true for entire disorders? Limited data suggest that nearly all personality disorders appear to cluster in families. The "odd" cluster disorders (paranoid, schizoid, and schizotypal) are particularly heritable, and it is common for individuals with one Cluster A disorder to have family members with other Cluster A disorders. Some research suggests that borderline personality disorder (BPD) may be due, at least in part, to heredity. Impulsivity and affective instability, both hallmarks of BPD, are behaviors that tend to run in families. Antisocial personality disorder is more common in first-degree relatives of those who have the disorder than of individuals without it. Determining genetic contribution is difficult, even if a disorder appears to run in families. Most families, in addition to sharing their genes, share their environment as well. Thus, sophisticated research methods, such as **twin studies**, are needed to determine to what extent family psychopathology is genetic versus environmental.

### PSYCHOLOGICAL INFLUENCES

Biology may build the foundation for personality disorders, but many researchers believe that psychological factors are crucial for their development. **Human cognition**—the processes by which we acquire, process, and retrieve information, may help explain how personality disorder symptoms develop and are maintained. In this next section, we will discuss

**Figure 5.1** Austrian physician and zoologist Konrad Lorenz (1903–1989). © *Bettmann/CORBIS*

three psychological factors—attachment, learning, and schemas—and how they contribute to personality disorder development.

## ATTACHMENT

The Austrian-born physician and zoologist Konrad Lorenz (1903–1989) was the first to study **imprinting behavior**. In birds, imprinting behavior is observed when the newborn baby observes and forms a strong bond with an object, usually its mother. This occurs shortly after birth in what is called the **critical period**. Although human infants do not exhibit imprinting exactly, they do show a wide range of complex **attachment behaviors**. In the 1950s the British psychoanalyst John Bowlby described attachment behaviors as those that are intended to keep the mother close to the child. By keeping the mother close, the infant is protected for the first year of life. S. J. Kirsh and J. Cassidy (1997)[7] argue that the infant develops an "internal working model" that is an idea of an attachment figure based on the availability and responsiveness of the attachment figure (usually the mother). These models have also suggested that attachment guides children's behavior, feelings, and processing of social information. This means that the relationship between the primary caregiver and the child serves as the foundation for future interpersonal relationships. Although attachment theorists have long suggested that attachment in infancy affects how children form relationships with other people, there are few studies that support this. However, some researchers believe that attachment patterns in infancy may be integral to the development of personality disorders in general, and borderline personality disorder specifically.[8]

## LEARNING

You have probably learned of Ivan Pavlov, the Russian physiologist who, in the 1890s, made an amazing discovery: Animals can learn to make associations between two events, a process he called **classical conditioning**. Classical conditioning occurs when an animal learns that something neutral, like a bell or a light, is

**Figure 5.2** Russian physiologist Ivan Pavlov with one of his dogs at a demonstration of the condition reflex phenomenon. © *Bettmann/CORBIS*

related to something desirable, like food. Pavlov presented dogs with meat and found that the dogs would drool. Then, Pavlov rang a bell and presented meat, and found once again, the dogs would drool. He repeated the pairings of the bell with the meat and then, after several repetitions, Pavlov rang the bell alone, without the meat. He found that when the bell was rung, the dogs still salivated, even though there was no meat. This showed that the dogs had learned that a ringing bell meant that meat was coming. We call the meat the **unconditioned stimulus (UCS)** because the dog would drool when the meat was presented alone, without the bell. The bell is called the **conditioned stimulus (CS)** because the animal is conditioned (trained) by repeated pairings of the bell with the meat that the bell means that meat is coming. Drooling when the meat is presented is called the **unconditioned response (UCR)** and drooling when the bell is rung without the meat is the **conditioned response (CR)**.

Pavlov's discovery teaches us that people can learn to attribute meaning to neutral events when they experience two events close together in time. Recall Theresa, who was in treatment for dependent personality disorder (see Chapter 4). As an adolescent, Theresa found her grandmother extremely controlling and critical. Her grandmother told her that she wasn't good enough to do things on her own, and sometimes even redid Theresa's homework. When Theresa tried to do things on her own, she became anxious and fearful. Although Theresa says she disliked her grandmother and eventually left home to get away from her, the feelings of helplessness that her grandmother fostered continued even after Theresa was married. She married a man quite a bit older than she was and allowed him to make all the decisions. When she was asked her opinion on a topic, she became anxious, recalling her feelings as a child. One might conclude that, from a young age, Theresa's attempts to be independent were thwarted by her controlling grandmother. When she completed a task on her own, her grandmother told her it wasn't good enough. Given these experiences, Theresa learned that she is helpless and must rely on the advice of others.

Classical conditioning is learning that occurs when a stimulus precedes a rewarding event (e.g., the bell that rings before the food is presented). However, it is not the only form of conditioned learning that may have a role in the development of personality disorders. In the 1950s, B. F. Skinner, a psychologist at Harvard University, observed that we engage in many behaviors because we receive a reward, or reinforcement, after the behavior takes place. For example, your parents might give you your allowance after you have completed your chores. In this case, you do your chores in order to receive your reward, your allowance. However, we also engage in behaviors in order to *avoid* certain negative consequences. Consider going to the dentist. Most people would not choose to go to the dentist just for

**Figure 5.3** Psychologist B.F. Skinner in 1933. © *Bettmann/CORBIS*

fun. However, if you do go to the dentist regularly, you may be able to avoid more invasive and painful dental procedures that result from tooth decay. According to the theory of **operant conditioning**, the likelihood that you will engage in a behavior increases if the consequence of that behavior is positive. Reinforcement occurs when a behavior is followed by an event that makes you want to repeat the behavior (like getting your allowance after doing your chores). There are three possible outcomes of behavior that make it likely that you will do it again: **positive reinforcement**, **negative reinforcement**, and **punishment**. Positive reinforcement occurs when something good happens after a behavior. For example, if you tell a joke and people laugh, you are receiving positive reinforcement for telling that joke. You are more likely to tell the same joke (or the same kind of joke) again. Negative reinforcement occurs when you do something in order to avoid or to stop something unpleasant. For example, when you take an aspirin to make a headache go away and feel better, you are likely to take aspirin the next time you have a headache, too. Finally, when a behavior elicits a negative consequence, such as getting grounded for staying out past your curfew, the negative consequence is called punishment. Effective punishment decreases the likelihood that one will engage in the same behavior again.

Principles of operant conditioning may be observed in action in several areas of mental illness. Consider Michele (see Chapter 4), who sought treatment for avoidant personality disorder. Michele is very uncomfortable around other people. She avoids most social interaction, going so far as to work at a nursery and spend most of her time tending the plants instead of being around people. The problem is, Michele spends so much time avoiding situations that make her anxious that she is unlikely to have experiences that change her negative expectations. She believes that social situations will only bring her pain—in her case, embarrassment or shame—so she avoids other people. Her avoidance limits her opportunities to learn that there are other possible outcomes to her behavior. If she took the promotion to assistant manager that her boss would like to award her, she might find that other people respect her opinion and value her knowledge about plants. If she has those positive experiences repeatedly, Michele might learn that social interaction doesn't always have to induce anxiety but, instead, can be quite rewarding. You may read more about how learning models are used for treating personality disorders in Chapter 6.

## SOCIAL LEARNING

Of course, you do not need to experience an event yourself in order to learn about what consequences follow certain behaviors. Albert Bandura, a researcher at Stanford University suggests that individuals actively seek out information about their environment to obtain favorable outcomes. When someone responds to a stimulus based upon an observation of another person's response, that is a result of **observational learning**. Sometimes, this form of learning can lead to positive behaviors. For example, while watching a Jim Carrey movie in a crowded theater, you might observe the power of comedy. That is, even though it is Jim Carrey who is making the audience laugh, you learn that by being funny, you can obtain attention and recognition, or put other people at ease, etc. This observation might lead you to work to improve your sense of humor. However, observing negative events can also have powerful effects. If your mother is repeatedly taken advantage of by her employer, you might become suspicious of other people. You might come to believe that people are out for themselves and that you need to be on guard to protect yourself, a trait associated with paranoid personality disorder. Although your mother is the one who is having the experience, the experience still influences you, through observational learning.

## SCHEMAS

A **cognitive theory** of mental disorders might add to our understanding of what causes and maintains personality disorder symptoms. A cognitive theory of mental disorders suggests that errors in thinking contribute to mental illness. A specific error in thinking, called a **schema**, is an underlying mental "map" that guides how we think about people and events. Someone who has a "depressive schema" might attend to, linger on, and remember negative information. Perhaps you know someone who is pessimistic, always expecting the worst. A person with a depressive schema might be extremely pessimistic, always looking on the bad side of things, seeking evidence to confirm his negative expectation. According to Aaron Beck, a professor of psychology at the University of Pennsylvania, this occurs because the person has a bias toward negative information.[9] This form of bias may be highly specialized or specific to a disorder or syndrome. For example, someone with paranoid personality disorder operates with a paranoid schema. Thus, he looks at all social information with an eye to detecting a threat (he knows it's in there somewhere). Someone with borderline personality disorder might have an "abandonment schema," making him or her particularly sensitive to cues of abandonment or betrayal.

## SOCIAL INFLUENCES

We have learned that heredity, or your family's genetic information, contributes to the development of personality disorders. In addition, psychological factors such as conditioning, social learning, and schemas might be factors in the development and maintenance of personality disorders. The last piece of the puzzle is made up of social, cultural, and interpersonal factors.

## SOCIOECONOMIC STATUS

There is a great divide in our society between the "haves" and the "have-nots." With poverty come several unique problems, including increased exposure to biological hazards, interpersonal violence, and limited access to medical and psychiatric care.

One personality disorder in which socioeconomic status must be considered is antisocial personality disorder.

Recall that antisocial personality disorder is largely described by a lifetime of unlawful behaviors such as theft, vandalism, and violence. These behaviors may begin at a very early age and continue into adulthood. Children who are raised in poverty are more likely to consume drinking water that has levels of lead high enough to cause mild or severe brain damage. Further, many children raised in poverty come from single-parent homes, in which there is limited parental supervision. Limited supervision increases the likelihood that a child will engage in antisocial behaviors and/or associate with other kids who frequently get in trouble. Getting in with the "wrong crowd" may lead to joining a gang, which introduces more illegal and violent behaviors. Indeed, according to the diagnostic criteria, many gang members may meet behavioral criteria for ASPD. There is significant debate in the field of psychology about whether ASPD should be considered a mental disorder because of the likelihood that life in impoverished urban areas sometimes leads to involvement in illegal activity. In other words, is it the person, or his response to his environment? We do know that antisocial behaviors are more common among people of low socioeconomic status. However, it is unclear how many of these individuals would continue to engage in antisocial behaviors if their environment were suddenly changed.

## GENDER

Gender roles have a strong effect on behavior in general and personality in particular. Just about everyone has an idea of appropriate gender-specific behavior. Even if you can't explain it, you can identify violations of gender roles. For males, violation of gender roles seems to come at a tremendous cost. Boys or men who behave in "feminine" ways are often labeled "weak."

Expressing emotion, while generally accepted in women, is often condemned in men. This may lead to differences between men and women in their willingness to seek help. Whereas a woman with depression might be comfortable telling her doctor about her feelings, a man might be more likely to "self-medicate" with alcohol or drugs. *Significantly, alcohol abuse and dependence is more common in men than women, while depressive disorders are more common in women than men.*

The impulsive personality disorders, or Cluster B, are disorders in which gender roles may be of particular influence. Women are more likely than men to be diagnosed with histrionic and borderline personality disorders, whereas men are more likely to be diagnosed with narcissistic and antisocial personality disorders. Some researchers have argued that this is unsurprising, considering that many of the diagnostic criteria involve extreme forms of behaviors that are common to one gender or the other.[12] This means that the disorders pathologize extreme variants of gender-related traits. Stereotypes of appropriate male behaviors include being strong, resourceful, and in control. An example of these attributes "gone bad" is when a person gets into frequent fights, is aggressive rather than assertive, and steals—behaviors that are consistent with antisocial personality disorder. Alternatively, stereotypes of appropriate female behaviors include being coy, flirtatious, and engaging. An example of a maladaptive version of these attributes occurs when one is vain, excessively seductive, or flamboyant, behaviors that are consistent with a diagnosis of histrionic personality disorder.

**INTERPERSONAL FACTORS: ABUSE AND NEGLECT**

As discussed earlier in this chapter, secure attachment in infancy provides, via interaction between mother and child, a model for appropriate social and emotional relationships. A loving family environment may help protect against a variety of mental disorders. However, what happens when there is extreme discord within the family? What happens when a child is exposed to domestic violence or emotional, physical, or sexual abuse? Some researchers believe that childhood abuse is one of the most important prerequisites for adult mental illness, particularly certain forms of personality pathology. Indeed, many people with borderline personality disorder report a history of childhood trauma, specifically physical and sexual abuse. (See endnotes 10–14.) Although physical and sexual abuse may contribute to personality disorders in adults, remember that abuse rarely occurs in a family that is otherwise functional and loving. Indeed, Joel Paris (1999) of McGill University in Montreal argues that childhood abuse is accompanied by various other pathological family attributes such as inadequate parenting and communication skills.[15] He believes that these qualities may be even more important than abuse itself.

### BIOPSYCHOSOCIAL PERSPECTIVE

Personality disorders may emerge from a combination of biological, psychological, and social factors. We have learned about a variety of these factors and looked at ways they might contribute to personality disorders. These factors rarely work in isolation. Instead, they combine and interact and may result in maladaptive behaviors. An excellent example of the biopsychosocial perspective in action is antisocial personality disorder. Recall Rick, Valerie's husband who cheated on her and gambled away their mortgage payment (see Chapter 3). Consider this information about Rick's childhood:

He was the youngest child in a family with two children. His mother, after being beaten by her husband for years, left their home just after Rick was born. She promised her sons that she would come back for them, but she never did. His father worked occasionally as a construction worker, when he could find the work, but otherwise spent his time at a local bar or at home watching television. Rick didn't feel like he knew his father. His father rarely spoke to Rick, except when he gave him orders. Rick's older brother, Sam, had a part-time job after school to help support the family. Sam was beaten repeatedly by his father, while Rick was virtually ignored.

The family lived in a small house on the outskirts of town. It was a fairly poor neighborhood, and there were no parks or community centers where the children could play in their free time. At the age of seven, Rick was allowed to come and go as he pleased and he spent a lot of time running around the neighborhood alone. Sometimes, he went to the corner store to get candy. Since he had no money, theft was his only option. He found that he enjoyed stealing. He figured that the storekeeper was old and stupid and deserved what he got.

When Rick was ten and in the fifth grade, he met Taylor and Tyler, twins who were in his class at school. Taylor was a controlling person with an active imagination for violence. Tyler generally went along with his brother's ideas and Rick was happy to join in. Together, the three boys vandalized the school, broke into houses, and tormented girls in class. Once, Taylor found an old, stray dog on their way home from school and ordered Rick and Tyler to join him in beating the dog. They proceeded to beat the dog to death and buried the dog in Rick's backyard. Eventually, Rick got expelled from school and was sent to a special school for children with behavioral problems. At his new school, there were plenty of other children who engaged in destructive behaviors, so Rick had no trouble finding new, equally deviant, friends. However, Rick was a bright student, and although he enjoyed breaking rules, he got good grades and eventually was sent to the public high school where he eventually met Valerie.

In considering Rick's childhood, it is easy to observe various biological, psychological, and social factors at play. Rick's father displays several antisocial traits. He abuses alcohol, is violent, and has trouble keeping a steady job. We don't know enough about him to be certain whether he has antisocial personality disorder but one can suppose that Rick inherited a predisposition for violent behavior. Further, Rick may have learned how to avoid being beaten by watching his brother Sam. Through observational learning, Rick learned that Sam, who worked hard at school and at his job, was punished at home by their father. Rick may have decided that hard work is rarely rewarded and that it is better to be the abuser than the victim. Finally, Rick grew up in poverty. His social environment insured that he had inadequate parenting and very little supervision. Chances are he ate a poor diet and had limited medical care. He made friends who had a similar lack of adult supervision who encouraged his deviant behavior.

**REVIEW**

Personality disorders emerge from a combination of biological, psychological, and social factors. Personality traits and, consequently, some personality disorders appear to run in families. In order to understand how personality disorders develop, it is necessary to take a biopsychosocial approach, considering the relationship among biological, psychological, and social factors in the development of a disorder.

# Treatment of
# Personality Disorders

**6**

**Just as it is difficult to pinpoint causes of personality disorders,** these disorders are very difficult to treat. By definition, personality disorders are chronic, pervasive, inflexible patterns of behavior that are resistant to change. Thus, by their nature, personality disorders present a challenge to mental health professionals.[13] People with personality disorders also often have more than one disorder. This **comorbidity** (a term introduced in the previous chapter) may affect how their treatment is designed and implemented.

Recall that people with personality disorders have many interpersonal problems. These problems will likely extend into a relationship with a therapist. For example, someone with paranoid or schizoid personality disorder has difficulty forming relationships and trusting other people. It would be particularly challenging for these patients to learn to trust the advice of their therapist. People with narcissistic or antisocial personality disorders usually do not see the problems with their behavior and, as a result, are unlikely to be interested in participating in therapy. Symptoms of borderline personality disorder include mood reactivity and inappropriate, intense anger. These qualities may disrupt therapy sessions and alienate mental health professionals. Some people with personality disorders are especially sensitive to criticism. Therapists treating these patients need to be especially careful not to put the patient on the defensive. Finally, people with dependent personality disorder are likely to rely on other people's opinions more than their own. Therapists who treat these people must beware of encouraging this dependency.

How does a therapist go about designing a treatment plan for a patient with a personality disorder? Usually, the therapist begins by identifying the goal or goals of treatment. There are several options:

1. Reduce the patient's distress
2. Minimize interpersonal problems
3. Increase the patient's awareness of his or her behaviors
4. Change behaviors
5. Change the structure of the patient's personality

A therapist might choose one or all of these as treatment goals when working with someone who has a personality disorder. The form of therapy they use depends upon the goal or goals of treatment. There are several approaches available. We will discuss three of these in the next section.

## THE BIOLOGICAL APPROACH

The biological approach to treating personality disorders is largely based on affecting the levels of or activity of certain **neurotransmitters**. Neurotransmitters are effectively the "messengers" of the brain, carrying information from one brain cell to another. Brain cells, called **neurons**, are sensitive to different kinds of neurotransmitters and have receptors built specifically for them. Neurons that are sensitive to specific neurotransmitters tend to cluster together, creating circuits in the brain that help spread information.

Neurotransmitters begin their journey in little sacs at the ends of neurons called the **presynaptic terminal**. An electric current,

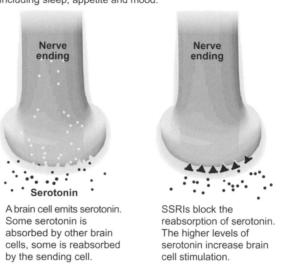

**Fine-tuning an anti-depressant**

The anti-depressant "selective serotonin re-uptake inhibitors", SSRIs, blocks the reabsorption of serotonin – a messenger chemical that is known to influence many of the brain's functions including sleep, appetite and mood.

Nerve ending

Nerve ending

Serotonin

A brain cell emits serotonin. Some serotonin is absorbed by other brain cells, some is reabsorbed by the sending cell.

SSRIs block the reabsorption of serotonin. The higher levels of serotonin increase brain cell stimulation.

SOURCE: Associated Press                              AP

**Figure 6.1** © *AP Images*

which begins in the nucleus of the neuron, is released down the **axon** and signals for the release of neurotransmitters. The little sacs open, and the neurotransmitters are released into the space between two neurons, called the **synapse**. In the synapse, the neurotransmitters attach, or bind, to the receptors at the ends of another neuron, thus affecting this new neuron. The new neuron takes in as much of the neurotransmitter as it can, then releases the excess. The excess is released back into the synaptic cleft and is reabsorbed by the first neuron, a process known as **reuptake**.

There are many different neurotransmitters in the brain. Two that have been found to be involved in causing personality disorder symptoms are **serotonin** and **dopamine**. Serotonin affects mood, behaviors, and thoughts. Low serotonin activity is associated with impulsive behaviors and unstable moods. Alternatively, high levels of serotonin have been associated with anxious or compulsive behaviors. Serotonin has been implicated in depression and may play a role in many personality disorders. Dopamine is primarily involved in movement and thoughts. Dopamine has also been associated with novelty-seeking, or interest in new experiences and rewards. Some illegal drugs, such as cocaine and methamphetamine, work by affecting dopamine function in the brain. Thus, dopamine is associated with feelings of pleasure and well-being. Dopamine pathways in the brain are highly specialized and may influence different kinds of thinking or behavior. People with high levels of dopamine in certain parts of the brain may experience psychotic symptoms or paranoid thinking, symptoms of "odd" cluster personality disorders. People with high levels of dopamine in other parts of the brain may be restless, always searching for fun and excitement. This kind of behavior is associated with antisocial personality disorder.

All medications for psychiatric conditions work by increasing or decreasing the availability or flow of certain neurotransmitters. Some drugs *block* production of a specific neurotransmitter. Others block neuron receptors, thus stopping the effect of the neurotransmitter. These drugs are called neurotransmitter **antagonists**. Another form of medication works by blocking reuptake. Blocking reuptake prevents the first neuron from taking back the extra neurotransmitter that was released into the synaptic cleft. This is how the most popular medications for depression work. Perhaps you have heard of the class of medications called **selective-serotonin reuptake inhibitors (SSRIs)**. The SSRIs have received a lot of attention in the media and have brand names like Prozac®, Paxil®, Wellbutrin®, and Zoloft®.

These medications work by increasing the amount of neuro-transmitter in the synapse that sends a signal to the receiving neuron. By increasing the amount of neurotransmitter, the neuron can then fire more frequently and increase the activity in brain circuits that are related to a sense of well-being.

The goal of the biological approach is to reduce the patient's distress and change behaviors. Some medications, such as the SSRIs, have been found to improve mood, thereby reducing anxiety and depression. An added benefit of these medications is that they can prevent harmful impulsive behaviors such as impulsive overeating, self-mutilation, and uncontrollable rage. Personality disorders that can be treated with these medications include borderline personality disorder, schizotypal personality disorder, dependent personality disorder, and avoidant personality disorder. There is another class of medications that affects dopamine activity. These drugs are used to treat schizophrenia and psychotic disorders. These medications are called anti-psychotic medications and can help reduce paranoid thinking and perceptual aberrations. They are sometimes used to treat "odd" cluster disorders such as schizoid, paranoid, and schizotypal personality disorders.

Historically, personality disorders were treated with psychotherapy exclusively. Current treatment often includes prescription medication, but medicine alone does not eliminate personality disorders. It might help treat the depression, anxiety, or paranoia associated with a personality disorder, but many symptoms require additional attention. This is why therapists generally use a form of psychotherapy in addition to medication.

## COGNITIVE APPROACH

One type of psychotherapy that has been somewhat effective in treating personality disorders is **cognitive-behavioral psychotherapy**, or **CBT**. CBT is used when the goals of treatment include: (1) increasing the patient's awareness of behaviors; (2) changing behaviors; (3) changing the structure of the patient's personality; and (4) minimizing interpersonal problems. The cognitive-behavioral approach to treating personality disorders is largely based on the assumption that the behaviors, attitudes, and beliefs of someone with a personality disorder are based upon faulty schemas (see Chapter 5). Schemas that are specific to personality disorders may cause a person to make errors in thinking or judgment that affect the way he or she views others and the world. For an example of a disorder-specific schema, consider Lynne, the patient with borderline personality disorder described in Chapter 3. Let's assume that Lynne has an "abandonment" schema. Because of this, she might tend to interpret people's behaviors as signs that they are planning to leave her. When her boyfriend Kevin went on a camping trip, Lynne assumed he was leaving to get away from her. In the past, when Lynne's mother left in order to visit her sister in another state, Lynne may have assumed that she wasn't coming back. A therapist using cognitive-behavioral therapy will attempt to identify these schemas, illuminate the faulty logic that is at their core, and, as a result, the problem behaviors.

## INTERPERSONAL PSYCHOTHERAPY
The interpersonal approach to treating mental disorders was first introduced by a clinical psychoanalyst, Harry Stack Sullivan (1953).[16] This approach assumes that early relationships, such as our relationships with our parents, lay the groundwork for future relationships. Thus, our earliest relationships may be played out again and again with our friends and loved ones. Interpersonal problems are a significant problem for people with personality disorders. Lorna Smith Benjamin[17], a psychologist at the University of Utah, applied the interpersonal

approach to treating personality disorders. She believes that if one can identify the faulty communication patterns that occurred in childhood, one can change the maladaptive patterns of communicating in adulthood. Consider Violet, the woman with a narcissistic personality disorder who was described in Chapter 3. Perhaps Violet's father was a successful president of a major corporation and was extremely authoritative and opinionated. Violet's father was frequently critical of her. He disparaged her attempts to impress him with papers she wrote for school or her athletic performance. He was equally critical of Violet's mother, who always gave in to her husband, assuming that his opinions were valid and ignoring or suppressing alternative perspectives. Perhaps Violet's father received similar attention from his employees and from other people in the community. Violet might have grown up with a low opinion of herself. Additionally, she might have learned that in order to be heard, one must be authoritative. She might also have learned to demand from others admiration similar to that her father received. Later in life, she might assume that others, like her husband, Mark, should also be considered extremely important and worthy of admiration. Given Violet's belief that she is superior to other people and deserves special attention, it is no surprise that she has significant difficulties in her life. Thus, the goal of interpersonal therapy for Violet would be to change her behaviors (her bossiness and unreasonable demands) and minimize her interpersonal problems (help her stop alienating people and make friends).

## TREATING SPECIFIC PERSONALITY DISORDERS

For the most part, little attention has been paid to the treatment of personality disorders. There are no sound controlled studies for the treatment of histrionic, narcissistic, schizoid, or paranoid personality disorders. Therapists do their best to adapt

# Mental health treatment on rise

Americans are seeking treatment for mental illness more frequently than they did 10 years ago. Health officials believe this may eventually decrease the overall rate of mental illness.

**Prevalence of mental disorders,** age 18 to 54

☐ 1990 to 1992
■ 2001 to 2003

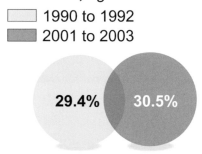

29.4%    30.5%

**Percentage of people with a disorder undergoing treatment**

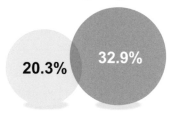

20.3%    32.9%

NOTE: Survey sampled 5,388 people in early 1990s and 4,319 from 2001 to 2003

SOURCES: National Institute of    AP
Mental Health; New England Journal
of Medicine

**Figure 6.2** © *AP Images*

general therapeutic strategies to help patients change their beliefs and behaviors that cause problems in their daily lives. Additionally, medications are sometimes used to minimize symptoms, and some forms of psychotherapy can be adapted for personality disorders. Borderline personality disorder and antisocial personality disorder have received substantial attention from researchers and specific treatment approaches have been designed for these disorders.

## TREATING BORDERLINE PERSONALITY DISORDER

In addition to medication, individuals with borderline personality disorder generally participate in some form of psychotherapy. A specific form of cognitive-behavioral therapy that is used to treat borderline personality disorder is **dialectical behavior therapy (DBT)**. This approach was developed by Marsha Linehan in the 1990s at the University of Washington and is designed to change behaviors and minimize interpersonal problems that may result from those behaviors.[18] Dialectical behavior therapy focuses on teaching patients to tolerate negative emotions without engaging in self-harming behaviors. Thus, the therapy focuses on minimizing behaviors that are harmful and that may interfere with treatment, such as cutting oneself, attempting suicide, missing therapy appointments, and going into the hospital. Patients in DBT have an individual therapist and also participate in group therapy sessions. Therapists are taught to understand and anticipate the destructive behaviors of individuals with BPD, but not to accept those behaviors.

Some research studies have suggested that DBT is effective in treating borderline personality disorder. In one study, borderline patients who received dialectical behavior therapy for one year were compared with patients who received another form of treatment. Both patient groups were followed for one year after treatment to compare how they were doing 12 months after completing treatment. Patients who received DBT engaged in fewer self-destructive and suicidal behaviors, reported less anger, missed fewer appointments with their therapists, and spent fewer days in the hospital than did the group who did not receive DBT. Although this is still a relatively new treatment, research suggests that it is a promising approach for treating borderline personality disorder.

## TREATING ANTISOCIAL PERSONALITY DISORDER
The biggest challenge in treating people with antisocial personality disorder is getting them in for treatment. These people do not experience distress, nor do they see their behaviors as problematic. Unfortunately, most treatment of individuals with ASPD takes place in prison settings. Rehabilitation is considered a crucial part of the penal system, but it is rarely effective. For one thing, it is extraordinarily expensive and, ultimately, taxpayers have to pay the bill. In addition, people with the kind of psychopathic traits that go hand-in-hand with antisocial personality disorder are especially resistant to treatment.

Some mental health professionals have taken a biological approach to treating ASPD. Mood stabilizers, such as lithium, which is traditionally used to treat bipolar disorder, are sometimes used for patients with ASPD. These medications are believed to minimize aggressive and impulsive behaviors, but there is little research supporting their effectiveness. Selective-serotonin reuptake inhibitors (SSRIs) and other antidepressants used for major depressive disorder and some personality disorders are occasionally used for antisocial personality disorder, but again, we know very little about whether or not they help. Features of ASPD make psychotherapy particularly challenging. ASPD sufferers are glib, callous, arrogant, and manipulative. They fail to see the harm they are doing to others and, when they do see it, they don't really care. As a result, psychotherapy designed to illuminate harmful behaviors does little good. These patients can't see why they shouldn't behave as they do and have little motivation to change.

There is some evidence that positive reinforcement for good behavior can serve as motivation for individuals with ASPD. Being part of a **token economy**, where good behavior is rewarded with some desired outcome such as money, food, or free time may increase the likelihood that the good behavior will be repeated. The problem is that token economies can only take place in a structured setting like therapy, a hospital, or a rehabilitation setting. Unfortunately, when the patient is out of treatment (or out of prison, as is likely the case for individuals with ASPD), there are fewer immediate rewards for good behavior. In the real world, the need to have patience and perseverance in order to reap the rewards for good behavior often proves too much of a challenge for these people.

## The Borderline Symptom Inventory (BSI)

This questionnaire was designed to help therapists and researchers measure the symptoms that a patient with borderline personality disorder experiences. The questionnaire asks patients about their mood, their thoughts, and their behaviors. The BSI can be used at each therapy session to help a clinician determine if and how the patient's symptoms are changing over time. Researchers can use the BSI to help them figure out if a patient is benefiting from treatment. Questionnaires like the Borderline Symptom Inventory have been very useful in helping mental health professionals learn more about symptoms of mental disorders.

Although there is limited information suggesting that ASPD and psychopathy can be treated, remember that research for this disorder is still in its earliest stages. Funding agencies are motivated to support research investigating treatment for ASPD because this disorder is such a drain on our economy. ASPD sufferers cause substantial harm to citizens and then cost taxpayers money to keep them in prison. It is in our best interest to figure out how best to treat ASPD in order to lower crime and prison populations.

## REVIEW

Treatment of personality disorders is particularly challenging. This is an extremely heterogeneous category of disorders that, by definition, are chronic, stable, and pervasive. Whereas there is little research investigating treatment effectiveness for most personality disorders, some attention has been paid to developing treatment strategies for borderline personality disorder and antisocial personality disorder. Individuals with antisocial personality disorder are particularly resistant to treatment, although new forms of therapy are being developed and tested, primarily in prisons. Treatment of personality disorders is still in its early stage. With time, funding, and increased awareness of these disorders, more effective and focused strategies should be designed.

# The Future of Personality Disorders

**There is still much that has to be learned about personality** disorders. We still need to know more about individual causes of each disorder and about what maintains or exacerbates symptoms, and to figure out whether and how personality disorders can be prevented. We need to design effective treatment strategies. All of these questions must be addressed using a biopsychosocial approach. That is, we must assume that these disorders originate and are maintained by biological, psychological, and social features that influence one another.

You may have noticed that scientists don't yet know a lot about some of these personality disorders. Whereas we seem to have lots of information about borderline or antisocial personality disorders, not much is known about histrionic or narcissistic personality disorders. Although we know that schizotypal personality disorder seems to be at least biologically related to schizophrenia and other psychotic disorders, we know very little about what causes schizoid or paranoid personality disorders. Researchers continue to study these disorders to help us learn more about what causes these disorders and how to prevent and treat them.

## WHAT IS THE PURPOSE OF A DIAGNOSIS?

The psychiatric community carefully constructs diagnostic categories for two reasons. First, diagnostic categories help clinicians identify patterns of behavior that guide treatment strategies. More practically, a diagnosis is used by health insurance companies to determine what benefits should be paid to whom. Second, diagnostic categories help establish a common language for researchers who are studying disorders. If scientists are able to group research participants into categories based on common symptoms, results from a study become meaningful. Scientists can conclude that research findings are particular to a group of people with a mental disorder in common. Without a predetermined description of symptoms, clinicians and health insurance companies have little direction in treating a patient, and information collected by researchers has little practical application.

Diagnostic categories are not unchangeable entities, however. As researchers collect more information, some symptoms may be removed from a diagnosis, and others added. Some diagnoses may even be eliminated altogether. Did you know that at one time, homosexuality was considered a mental disorder? Research on the prevalence of homosexual behavior and changing cultural values persuaded the psychiatric community to reconsider its categorization of homosexuality as disordered and remove it from the diagnostic manual in 1973. Similarly, some personality disorder diagnostic categories have changed, been eliminated, or will be added in the future.

Sometimes, researchers conclude that some diagnoses should be considered **provisional categories**, or categories that require further study before they are included in the diagnostic manual. There are two such personality disorders: depressive and passive-aggressive personality disorders. People with depressive personality disorder have a gloomy, depressive interpretation of life. They may feel that they don't deserve to have fun or to relax. These people might be considered **pessimistic**. Someone with passive-aggressive personality disorder is negative and resists other people's demands to get work done or function at the expected level. These people complain that they are misunderstood, cheated, and unappreciated. People with passive-aggressive personality disorder have difficulty with authority figures. They are often critical and hostile toward teachers or employers and may blame others for their own mistakes.

Provisional categories establish guidelines for researchers. As researchers collect more information about a provisional category, they determine whether the category should indeed be considered an established diagnosis, or whether its symptoms are better accounted for by another condition.

## YOU ARE THE PSYCHOLOGIST: WHAT PERSONALITY DISORDER DOES RON HAVE?

Now that you have read about the symptoms of each personality disorder, it's time to practice your diagnostic skills. The work of a psychologist is much like the work of a detective. First, a psychologist wants to learn a person's story. Their narrative, or description of their life, can give a therapist a good idea of what a patient has experienced and what this individual thinks about their social and work environments. A psychologist must ask questions to determine patterns of behaviors. They must find out what effect these behaviors have on the patient or other people. They need to learn what kind of discomfort the patient is experiencing in order to figure out how best to help them. Read the case study of Ron and see if you can identify some personality disorder symptoms. Write them down as you go along, and ask yourself what questions you need to answer before you make a diagnosis.

**CASE STUDY**

Ronald is a news anchor for a television station in San Diego, California. He is very successful, and would very much like to be an anchor for a network in New York. In fact, Ron is convinced that he will one day work for a big network. Ron has always wanted to be the center of attention. When he was a child, he would put on plays for his family and neighbors and he would get angry if they weren't giving him enough attention. It was not uncommon for him to throw temper tantrums in public, a habit that his mother particularly disliked. As an adult, it seems that Ron has found his niche; he has tens of thousands of people watching him every day and he conveys information with authority.

Ron has had some problems at work, problems that his producers are generally able to overlook because Ron is popular with the viewers. To begin, Ron is choosing clothes that are more and more outlandish. His suits are often brightly colored with patterns that look terrible on television. He is arrogant and haughty, and treats other people at the station as if they are not as important as he. Veronica, a new female anchor at the station, is a new interest of Ron's. Indeed, Ron has engaged in some inappropriate sexually aggressive behaviors to get her attention. On one occasion, Ron called Veronica and asked her to come to his office for a meeting. When she arrived, she found Ron with his shirt off, lifting weights; an obvious and pitiful attempt at flirtation.

Veronica decided to go out with Ron despite his embarrassing attempts to get her attention. When they went out, Ron purported to be an expert on several topics, about which he obviously knew nothing. He spoke in a grandiose, theatrical manner. Later that same evening, Ron pulled a flute out of his suit and gave a performance for the entire restaurant. Still, Veronica found that she liked him. After one date, she was interested in getting to know him more. Clearly, Ron felt the same way because after one date, he announced on the news that they were in love. Veronica and the station managers are frustrated and embarrassed by Ron's behaviors. Ron, however, has no idea why everyone is upset.

---

**YOU ARE THE PSYCHOLOGIST: WHAT IS RON'S DIAGNOSIS?**
Ron sounds like a real pain in the neck! He is haughty, inappropriate, and always wants to be the center of attention. These traits may remind you of two personality disorders, narcissistic and histrionic personality disorders. Ron definitely shows some features of narcissistic personality disorder. He is arrogant and has a grandiose sense of his own importance. He might require excessive admiration, but from the description, we only know that he requires excessive attention, a feature associated with histrionic personality disorder. To receive a diagnosis of histrionic personality disorder, Ron must exhibit at least five symptoms of the disorder. Let's see if he does.

1. Ron is uncomfortable in situations in which he is not the center of attention. In fact, he has exhibited this behavior since childhood. His chosen career provides him the stage that he has always desired: He has thousands of people watching him daily.
2. Ron's interaction with Veronica is inappropriately sexual and seductive. When he invites her into his office to see him flexing his muscles, he is acting provocatively.
3. Ron consistently uses his physical appearance to draw attention to him. He dresses flamboyantly, in colorful suits that are in contrast to what he should wear on television.
4. Ron is extremely dramatic and theatrical. When he took Veronica to the bar, he came prepared for a flute performance! Somehow, he managed to hide his flute in his jacket.

5. Ron considers relationships to be more intimate than they actually are. After one date with Veronica, Ron announced to all of San Diego that they were in love.

Ron indeed exhibits at least five symptoms of histrionic personality disorder and two features of narcissistic personality disorder. The next step for a psychologist is to decide if these examples indicate a pervasive pattern of behaviors that are consistent with a personality disorder diagnosis. Has Ron been overly seductive with other women? Is he likely to become angry if others are not attending to him? Does he dress flamboyantly

## How Do You Tell If Someone Has a Personality Disorder?

The work of mental health professionals can be very challenging. When someone comes to a therapist for treatment, the therapist must consider several possible explanations for the patient's behavior before making a diagnosis. The process of ruling out other diagnoses is called making a differential diagnosis. This is a description of a sample differential diagnosis for antisocial personality disorder:

1. Is the patient at least 18 years old?

2. Does the patient have a history of antisocial acts, or conduct disorder before age 15?

3. Does the patient have a substance use disorder?
   If yes, does the patient engage in antisocial acts that are not related to their substance use disorder (for example, stealing things unrelated to drug use)?

when he is not at work? If so, treatment goals should be identified and a treatment plan designed.

This description of Ron may have sounded familiar to you. (In fact, it is loosely based on the movie *Anchorman*, starring Will Ferrell.) Now that you have an understanding about what personality disorders are, you will no doubt notice features of these disorders in characters in books, movies, and television shows. When you watch the news or read a newspaper, you may wonder if certain politicians or movie stars have personality disorders. Sometimes these symptoms are funny; more often they are upsetting and cause great discomfort and interfere

4. Is the patient arrogant, selfish, and haughty?

   If yes, is he or she also impulsive or aggressive? Arrogance without impulsivity or aggression might be better characterized by narcissistic personality disorder.

5. Does the patient manipulate others to gain power or profit or attention?

   If manipulative behaviors are not used to obtain material gain, consider borderline personality disorder.

6. Does the patient engage in criminal behaviors?

   If so, are these behaviors accompanied by the personality characteristics associated with antisocial personality disorder?

A therapist will use these kinds of questions in order to consider all diagnostic possibilities for a patient. Once they have eliminated several diagnoses, a final diagnosis (or more than one) will be assigned.

with people's lives. Whatever the case may be, personality disorders are serious mental disorders that require attention and treatment.

By reading this book, you have learned about some of the most interesting types of mental disorders. Personality disorders are not common. In general, they affect only about 1 percent of the population of the United States. Other than people with borderline personality disorder, individuals with personality disorders rarely seek treatment. This is because these people feel that their disorder is a part of them, something unlikely to be changed. As yet, unfortunately, this is true. We know very little about how to treat personality disorders and even less about how to prevent them. This will not change until more individuals with these problems are brought to the attention of mental health professionals. Many people do not want to see a therapist for their problems because there is a **stigma** in our society associated with getting help for mental illness. That is, people sometimes believe that they should be able to get over their problems on their own and that, by seeking help, they are admitting weakness. Motion picture mogul Samuel Goldwyn once quipped, "Anyone who goes to see a psychiatrist ought to have his head examined," which sums up some people's uninformed views of seeking treatment for mental health. Additionally, people with personality disorders may avoid asking for help because of the very nature of their disorder. They may be very uncomfortable around others and thus avoid interaction. They might have difficulty trusting others and so not want to tell someone else about their problems. Finally, they might not believe that they have a problem. Instead, they may believe that any problems in their lives are caused by the behavior of other people.

Researchers around the world are working daily to collect more information about personality disorders. Their job will not end until personality disorders are eradicated entirely—an unlikely outcome. Until then, we can hope to learn more about what causes these disorders and how we can help the people who suffer from them.

# NOTES

1. Costa, P. T., Jr., and R. R. McCrae. "Personality Disorders and the Five-Factor Model of Personality." *Journal of Personality Disorders* 4 (1990): 362–371.

2. Lenzenweger, M.F., and R.G. Dworkin, eds. *Origins and Development of Schizophrenia: Advances in Experimental Psychopathology*. Washington D.C.: American Psychological Association, 1998.

3. Widiger, T. A., A. J. Frances, H. A. Pincus, W. W. Davis, and M. B. First. "Toward an Empirical Classification for the *DSM-IV*." *Journal of Abnormal Psychology* 100 (1991): 280–288.

4. Kagan, J. *Galen's Prophesy*. New York: Basic Books, 1994.

5. Schwartz, C. E., N. Snidman, and J. Kagan. "Early Childhood Temperament as a Determinant of Externalizing Behavior in Adolescence." *Developmental Psychopathology* 8 (1996): 527–537.

6. Schwartz, C.E., N. Snidman, and J. Kagan. "Adolescent Social Anxiety as an Outcome of Inhibited Temperament in Childhood." *Journal of the American Academy of Adolescent Psychiatry* 38 (1999): 1008–1015.

7. Kirsh, S.J., and J. Cassidy. "Preschoolers' Attention to and Memory for Attachment Relevant Information." *Child Development* 68 (1997): 1143–1153.

8. Baird, A. A., H. B. Veague, and C. E. Rabbitt. "Developmental Precipitants of Borderline Personality Disorder." *Development and Psychopathology* 17 (2005): 1–19.

9. Beck, A.T., and A. Freeman, and associates. *Cognitive Therapy of Personality Disorders*. New York: Guilford, 1990.

10. Browne, A., and D. Finkelhor. "Impact of Child Sexual Abuse: A Review of the Research." *Psychological Bulletin* 99 (1986): 66–77.

11. Herman, J. L., J. C. Perry, and B. A. van der Kolk. "Childhood Trauma in Borderline Personality Disorder." *American Journal of Psychiatry* 146 (1989): 490–495.

12. Westen, D., P. Ludolph, B. Misle, S. Ruffins, and J. Block. "Physical and Sexual Abuse in Adolescent Girls with Borderline Personality Disorder." *American Journal of Orthopsychiatry* 60 (1990): 55–66.

13. Zanarini, M. C., J. G. Gunderson, M. F. Marino, E. O. Schwartz, and F. R. Frankenburg. "Childhood Experiences of Borderline Patients." *Comprehensive Psychiatry* 30 (1989): 18–25.

14. Zanarini, M. C., A. A. Williams, R. E. Lewis, D. B. Reich, S. C. Vera, M. F. Marino. "Reported Pathological Childhood Experiences Associated with the Development of Borderline Personality Disorder." *American Journal of Psychiatry* 154 (1997): 1101–1106.

15. Paris, J. "Borderline Personality Disorder." In T. Millon, P. H. Blaney, and R. D. David, eds. *Oxford Textbook of Psychopathology* (pp.628–652). New York: Oxford University Press, 1999.

16. Sullivan, H. S. *The Interpersonal Theory of Psychiatry*. New York: Norton, 1953.

17. Benjamin, L. S. *Interpersonal Diagnosis and Treatment of Personality Disorders*. New York: Guilford, 1999.

18. Linehan, M. M. *Cognitive-Behavioral Treatment of Borderline Personality Disorder: The Dialectics of Effective Treatment*. New York: Guilford, 1993.

**agoraphobia**—Fear of being in places or situations from which escape would be difficult or embarrassing.

**antagonist**—A type of medication that blocks the flow or activity of a neurotransmitter.

**antipsychotic medications**—Drugs that affect dopamine activity and minimize psychotic symptoms such as paranoid thinking, hallucinations, and delusions.

**antisocial personality disorder**—Disorder characterized by frequent violation of the rights of others.

**attachment behaviors**—Actions that are performed by the child that are intended to keep the caregiver close to the child.

**avoidant personality disorder**—Disorder characterized by a fear of being criticized, embarrassed, or appearing foolish.

**axis system**—Way to categorize mental disorders by grouping the disorders based on their shared characteristics or qualities.

**axon**—The part of a neuron, or brain cell, down which the electric current travels.

**behaviorally inhibited**—In infants, a style of temperament in which the baby is significantly fearful of new situations.

**behaviorally uninhibited**—Refers to a style of temperament in infants in which infants show little fear in new situations.

**biopsychosocial approach**—A way in which researchers consider biological, psychological, and social influences when describing mental disorders.

**borderline personality disorder**—A disorder characterized by unstable moods, impulsive behaviors, and stormy relationships.

**clairvoyance**—The ability to perceive things not apparent to the ordinary senses, sometimes including an ability to see the future. A claim of clairvoyance is symptomatic of schizotypal personality disorder.

**classical conditioning**—A type of learning in which a neutral stimulus (for example, a bell) is paired with a meaningful stimulus (such as food) until it elicits a response (such as salivation). See also *conditioned response, stimulus*.

**clusters**—The three groups of personality disorders included in the Diagnostic and Statistical Manual of mental disorders.

**Cluster A**—Personality disorders characterized by "odd" or "weird" thinking (e.g., paranoid, schizoid, and schizotypal personality disorders).

**Cluster B**—Personality disorders characterized by impulsive behaviors (e.g., antisocial, borderline, histrionic, and narcissistic personality disorders).

**Cluster C**—Personality disorders characterized by anxious behaviors (e.g., avoidant, dependent, and obsessive-compulsive personality disorders).

**cognitive behavioral therapy (CBT)**—A type of psychotherapy that focuses on identifying and changing thoughts, beliefs, and attitudes that contribute to mental disorders.

**cognitive distortions**—Strange ways of perceiving and thinking about the world characteristic of paranoid, schizoid, and schizotypal personality disorders.

**comorbidity**—The occurrence of more than one mental disorder at the same time in the same person.

**conditioning**—A process of learning that occurs after repeated experiences.

**conditioned response**—See *response, conditioned.*

**conditioned stimulus**—See *stimulus, conditioned.*

**conduct disorder**—A disorder that occurs in childhood in which a child shows a pattern of misbehavior and aggressive acts. A diagnosis of conduct disorder in childhood is required of adults diagnosed with antisocial personality disorder.

**critical period**—The time in infancy during which a baby bonds with its parent or other attachment figure.

**dependent personality disorder**—A personality disorder in which the affected individual has difficulty making decisions and engages in clinging behavior to ensure that others will take care of him or her.

**depressive personality disorder**—A personality disorder in which the person is frequently sad and pessimistic.

**diagnosis**—A conclusion about the kind(s) of mental disorder a patient has.

**differential diagnosis**—The process by which a mental health professional considers and rules out many diagnoses before assigning a final diagnosis.

**dissociation** (*verb*: **dissociate**)—A psychological mechanism through the human mind that cuts off thoughts or memories that cause anxiety.

**dopamine**—A neurotransmitter that is involved in symptoms of schizophrenia as well as schizoid, paranoid, and schizotypal personality disorders.

**emotional dysregulation**—A hallmark of borderline personality disorder in which an individual's understanding, experience, and expression of emotion is unstable and often inappropriate.

**heritable**—Able to be passed down from generation to generation.

**heterogeneity**—Variety within a group.

**histrionic personality disorder**—A disorder in which an individual wants to always be the center of attention and acts in ways that ensure that others are always looking at him or her.

**idea of reference**—A psychotic symptom in which an individual believes that something in the environment has special meaning. For example, someone who sees a pattern in the bark of a tree or the shape of a cloud may believe that it is a message from God.

**idiosyncratic**—Unique to a specific individual.

**imprinting behavior**—An infant's development of a bond to its parent or other attachment figure.

**impulsivity**—Engaging in a behavior without thought or consideration of the consequences. A symptom of borderline and antisocial personality disorders.

**insight**—The ability to understand one's illness or the meanings of one's behavior.

**magnetic resonance imaging (MRI)**—A noninvasive technique, similar to using an X-ray machine by which physicians are able to examine brain structure and function using magnetic fields.

**major depressive disorder**—A form of mental illness in which an individual experiences periods of clinical depression lasting longer than two weeks and occurring more than once.

**narcissistic personality disorder**—A personality disorder marked by a sense that one is superior to others and deserves special treatment.

**narrative**—The story that someone tells to describe his or her life experience.

**negative reinforcement**—See *reinforcement, negative.*

**neuron**—Brain cell.

**neurotic**—Refers to thoughts or behaviors that are not psychotic but are due to excessive and unrealistic anxiety.

**neurotransmitter**—A chemical messenger of the brain. Neurotransmitters are substances that are passed from one neuron to another and thus affect brain activity.

**nucleus**—The central part of a cell where the chromosomes or genetic information are stored.

**observational learning**—Learning from watching someone else experience an event.

**obsessive-compulsive disorder**—A disorder that is characterized by unwanted thoughts (obsessions) and/or behaviors that one feels the need to perform again and again (compulsions).

**obsessive-compulsive personality disorder**—A personality disorder in which someone pays so much attention to details and organization that he or she has difficulty completing tasks.

**operant conditioning**—Occurs when someone learns how to respond to an event based upon whether he or she receives punishment or reward.

**overvalued ideas**—Nonpsychotic ideas that a person believes, despite evidence to the contrary. An example of an overvalued idea is the belief that one's husband is cheating, even if there is no reasonable evidence that this is so.

**paranoid personality disorder**—A personality disorder marked by suspiciousness and paranoia.

**passive-aggressive personality disorder**—A personality disorder in which someone resists social and work demands by working slowly or being argumentative and sulking.

**pathologize**—To consider someone's behavior a symptom of mental disorder rather than a normal response to an environmental circumstance.

**perceptual alterations**—A symptom of schizotypal personality disorder in which someone sees or hears something in their environment and interprets it as having special meaning for them. For example, someone who hears the wind blowing and hears his or her name in the wind is having a perceptual alteration.

**persecutory delusions**—A psychotic symptom in which the victim believes that someone or something is out to get him or her.

**personality disorder**—A category of mental disorder characterized by personality characteristics that cause problems in a person's career and personal life.

**pessimistic**—Having a negative outlook, expecting the worst, "seeing the glass as half empty."

**positive reinforcement**—See *reinforcement, positive.*

**presynaptic terminal**—The place at the end of the neuron where the neurotransmitter is released.

**provisional category**—A group of disorders being considered along with other disorders in the diagnostic manual of the American Psychiatric Association (APA).

**psychotic**—Thoughts or behaviors that are clearly not based in reality, such as hearing or seeing things that aren't there.

**punishment**—A negative event that decreases the likelihood that a behavior will occur again.

**qualitative**—Referring to the kind or quality of something.

**quantitative**—Referring to the amount or measurement of something.

**range of affect**—The ability to display a variety of emotions.

**reinforcement**—Something that occurs following a behavior that affects the likelihood that that behavior will be repeated.

**reinforcement, negative**—A form of reinforcement in which one engages in a behavior in order to end a negative experience. For example, taking an aspirin to make a headache go away is a form of negative reinforcement.

**reinforcement, positive**—Rewarding a behavior with something desirable in order to increase the likelihood that that behavior will occur again.

**response, conditioned (CR)**—A learned response that happens after repeated exposure to a conditioned stimulus. See also *classical conditioning.*

**response, unconditioned (UCR)**—The naturally occurring response to a stimulus. For example, dogs salivate when meat is presented.

**reuptake**—A process by which one neuron releases a neurotransmitter, which then attaches to another neuron. The second neuron then releases the excess neurotransmitter, which is then taken back by the first neuron.

**sac**—The place at the end of neurons where neurotransmitters are held before being released into the synapse.

**schema**—A system of thoughts and beliefs that affects how someone views others and the world.

**schizoid personality disorder**—A personality disorder in which someone is detached from other people and prefers to be alone.

**schizotypal personality disorder**—A personality disorder in which someone experiences minor perceptual alterations, superstitious beliefs, and ideas of reference.

**selective-serotonin reuptake inhibitors (SSRIs)**—A class of antidepressant medications that work by blocking the reuptake of serotonin, thus increasing the amount of serotonin that remains in the synapse, or synaptic cleft.

**serotonin**—A neurotransmitter that is involved in causing the depressive and anxious symptoms that are part of several personality disorders.

**splitting**—A symptom of borderline personality disorder in which someone cannot maintain conflicting or nuanced views of someone and instead sees people as either all good or all bad.

**stereotypes**—Beliefs and assumptions about groups of people based upon shared group characteristics such as political affiliation or ethnic identification.

**stigma**—Negative characteristics attributed by others to one who possesses certain qualities or belongs to a certain group; in this context a negative view of people experiencing mental illness in general that may not be based on fact.

**stimulus, conditioned (CS)**—A previously neutral stimulus (such as a bell) that, after repeated pairings with a meaningful stimulus (such as food), develops the power to elicit a conditioned response.

**stimulus, unconditioned (UCS)**—Something that, by itself, elicits a response. For example, food is an unconditioned stimulus that naturally elicits salivation.

**synapse**—The space between two neurons where neurotransmitter exchange takes place. Also known as the synaptic cleft.

**temperament**—The foundation of adult personality as seen in infants.

**token economy**—A therapeutic environment, sometimes used to treat anti-social personality disorder, in which good behaviors are rewarded with money, food, or some other desired outcome.

**twin studies**—Research design that uses human twins to study the influence of genes or environment on mental disorders.

**unconditioned response**—See *response, unconditioned.*

**unconditioned stimulus**—See *stimulus, unconditioned.*

# FURTHER READING

American Psychiatric Association. *Diagnostic and Statistical Manual of Mental Disorders*, 4th ed. Washington, D.C.: American Psychiatric Association, 2000.

Butcher, J. N., S. Mineka, and J. M. Hooley. *Abnormal Psychology*. Boston: Pearson, 2004.

Garland, Jane E. *Depression Is the Pits, but I'm Getting Better: A Guide for Adolescents*. Washington, D.C.: Magination Press, 1997.

Hare, R.D. *Without Conscience: The Disturbing World of the Psychopath Among Us*. New York: Pocket Books, 1993.

Morrison, J. *DSM-IV Made Easy: The Clinician's Guide to Diagnosis*. New York: Guilford, 1995.

Patterson, Anna. *Running on Empty: A Novel about Eating Disorders for Teenage Girls*. London: Paul Chapman Educational Publishing, 2002.

Raskin, Rachel. *Feeling Better: A Kid's Book about Therapy*. Washington, D.C.: Magination Press, 2005.

Sones, Sonya. *Stop Pretending: What Happened When My Big Sister Went Crazy*. New York: HarperCollins, 2001.

**Borderline Personality Disorder Resource Center**

http://www.bpdresourcecenter.org

**Laboratory for Adolescent Science at Dartmouth College**

http://www.theteenbrain.com

**National Alliance for the Mentally Ill**

http://www.nami.org

**National Institute of Mental Health**

http://www.nimh.nih.gov

**National Mental Health Association**

http://www.nmha.org

**Neuroscience for Kids**

http://staff.washington.edu/chudler/neurok.html

# INDEX

inhibition, 50
insight, 9, 103
interpersonal psychotherapy, 84–85
interpersonal relationships
abuse and neglect as cause of disorders, 75–76
and anxious personality disorders, 49
attachment behaviors, 67
and BPD, 39
and Cluster A disorders, 28
and Cluster B disorders, 29
and HPD, 33
and NPD, 38
and PPD, 15–16
and relationship with therapist, 79–80
and SPD, 21
and treatment, 79–80

Kagan, J., 64
Kirsch, S. J., 67

language, for researchers, 92
language, idiosyncratic, 25
language, vague, 33
latent schizophrenia. *See* schizotypal personality disorder
Lenzenweger, Mark, 27
lithium, 88
Lorenz, Konrad, 66, 67
lying, 46
"Lynne" (BPD case study), 39–40, 84

magnetic resonance imaging (MRI), 27, 103
major depressive disorder, 103
males. *See* men
marriage, 15. *See also* romantic relationships
medication. *See* biological approach to treatment
men
and ASPD, 46, 48

gender roles, 74–75
and NPD, 34
and OCPD, 61
and PPD, 19
and SPD, 19
and specific personality disorders, 12
and STPD, 26
mental disorders, prevalence of, 2
methamphetamine, 82
"Michael" (STPD case study), 23–24
"Michele" (APD case study), 50–51, 71–72
mood stabilizers, 88
moralism, 59
MRI. *See* magnetic resonance imaging
multiple diagnoses, 63
murder, 47
mutilation. *See* self-mutilation

narcissistic personality disorder (NPD), 34–38, 103
and interpersonal therapy, 85
and patient-therapist relationship, 79
symptoms, 12
narrative, 104
negative emotions, 87
negative reinforcement. *See* reinforcement, negative
negative self-image, 50
neglect, 75–76
neuron, vi, viii, 80, 104
neurotic/neuroticism, 3, 64, 104
neurotransmitter, vi, 80–83, 104
neurotransmitter antagonist. *See* antagonist
novelty-seeking behavior, 82
NPD. *See* narcissistic personality disorder
nucleus, 104

observational learning, 72, 104
obsessive-compulsive disorder (OCD), 56, 104

schizophrenia, 14–15, 26–27

schizotypal personality disorder (STPD),
    22–28, 106
    "Donald" (example), 14
    and old borderline personality disorder
        definition, 38
    schizophrenia and, 26–27
    symptoms, 12

schizotype, 26–27

selective serotonin reuptake inhibitors
    (SSRIs), 81–83, 88, 106

self-criticism, 59

self-medication, 75

self-mutilation, 42, 87

serotonin, 81, 82, 106

sexual abuse, 76

sexually aggressive behavior, 34

sexually provocative behavior, 31, 33

shyness, 21

single-parent homes, 74

Skinner, B. F., 69, 70

social cues, 25

social influences, 73–76

social learning, 72

socioeconomic status, 73–74

sociopath, 43

SPD. See schizoid personality disorder

splitting, 41–42, 106

SSRIs. See selective serotonin reuptake
    inhibitors

stable disorders, 10

stereotypes, 106

"Steven" (PPD case study), 16–17

stigma, 98, 106

stimulus, conditioned (CS), 68, 106

stimulus, unconditioned (UCS), 68, 107

STPD. See schizotypal personality
    disorder

stress, 41

suicide attempts, 42, 87, 88

Sullivan, Harry Stack, 84

superstition, 24

suspiciousness, 18

synapse, vi, 81, 83, 107

tantrums, 33, 40

tasks, starting/completing, 54–56

temperament, 64–65, 107

theft, ASPD and, 77

therapist, relationship with, 79–80

therapy, avoiding, 52, 75, 98

therapy, seeking, 31

"Theresa" (DPD case study), 53–54, 69

"3 W's," 11

token economy, 89, 107

treatment, of personality disorders,
    79–90

trust, in patient-therapist relationship, 79

twin studies, 65, 107

type A personalities, 59, 60

unconditioned response (UCR). See
    response, unconditioned

unconditioned stimulus (UCS). See stim-
    ulus, unconditioned

unlawful behavior, ASPD and, 44–48, 90

vanity, NPD and, 34

"Violet" (NPD case study), 34–37, 85

Wellbutrin®, 82

Widiger, Thomas, 63

women
    and BPD, 34, 43
    gender roles, 75
    and HPD, 34
    and specific personality disorders, 12

workaholism, OCPD and, 56

Zoloft®, 82

# AUTHOR

**Heather Barnett Veague** attended the University of California, Los Angeles and received her Ph.D. in psychology from Harvard University in 2004. She is the author of several journal articles investigating information processing and the self in borderline personality disorder. Currently, she is working on a book with Dr. Abigail Baird about insight into adolescent behavior informed by evolution and neuroscience. Dr. Veague lives in Stockbridge, Massachusetts with her husband and two-year-old daughter.